Good Seed and Zizania

—⁂—

And Other Sermons and Writings

+John S. Thornton

ISBN: 1533574855

ISBN: 9781533574855

For permissions or reprint information,
please contact jsthornton32@gmail.com

Edited by Stuart Hotchkiss

Front cover illustration by Nancy Lindburg

Printed in the USA

Table of Contents

Dedication

This book is dedicated to my wife, Janylee,

and to our children,

John Thornton, Jr.

Andrea Thornton

Scott Sommer

Julia (Sommer) Ramirez

Introduction

After publishing two collections of sermons (*The Backside of God* and *Consider the Lilies*), I expected this to be yet another and, probably, the last. As it turns out, it is and it isn't. There are sermons that I preached in Episcopal churches in Idaho (Boise, Hailey and Sun Valley) and Oregon (Eugene and Salem) as well as one I preached in Texas (Wimberley). I've included the homilies I preached for the blessing of couples who were entering into life-long covenants, one for a man and a woman, one for two men. Then I decided to add the eulogy I preached at the memorial service for my friend and former parishioner Erik Erikson, the well-known psychoanalyst and author (*Childhood and Society, Young Man Luther, Gandhi's Truth*, etc.). That was in 1994, in the community church in the village of Harwich on Cape Cod. Sometime in the middle of the '80s, I wrote an article about the family farm crisis in the U.S., titled "Between Harvest and Winter," which was published in *The Oregon Episcopalian*. I've always liked that article and don't want it to get lost in a pile of papers; so it's here too. While digging through a box-full of sermons and newsletters, there it was, the poem that was published in *Episcopal Life*, the National Church's monthly publication years ago. It's titled "Did You See Him in the '60s?" It's passionate and, typically, sassy. The publication date had to have been sometime at the end of the '60s or in the early '70s. Finally, I had an urge to share a journal I kept when I went to see a dying friend in England, an historian and theologian named Donald Nicholl. He phoned one day to say, "John, I'm dying." I said, "I'm coming to see you." It was a journey I had to take. With his books (*Holiness, The Testing of Hearts, Triumphs of the Spirit in Russia*, etc.) and his personality, he had, as few others, formed me as a follower of the Christ.

I realized that the book of sermons had become a kind of retrospective. There was something from the '60s, something from the '80s, something from the '90s, all the rest from 2015 and 2016. You may get an idea of who I've been and who I've become and how I've tried to be faithful to the Gospel of Jesus Christ, imperfectly, of course. As I approach the end of life – hoping the very end won't come for a decade or more – I'd like the world to know this much about me. It's my way of saying, Here I stand.

At the very end of the book is "A Blessing," with which I've blessed confirmands over the years. Vicariously, I bless you, too. Please note the attribution at the bottom of the page.

I was unable to find the collection of letters to editors regarding capital punishment, however. I want everyone to know that I consider the execution of persons to be an uncivilized and barbaric practice. By killing persons, the state kills its moral authority. I hope, some day, to find those letters and publish them.

Producing even a small book isn't a one-person effort. The author has to rely on the skills of others, especially the skill of friendship. Just when the author's enthusiasm and determination peter out, along comes someone who reinvigorates the whole process. To the end of my days, I will be grateful to Gail Collins, John Greenfield's secretary at Huntley Law in Boise, Idaho. Gail re-typed and formatted every sermon and article in this collection – and with hardly believable speed and accuracy. The person who came along to reinvigorate the process was Stuart Hotchkiss, a faithful friend (and the groom in "Stuart and Lisa at the Blessing of Their Covenant"). He brought it all to the verge of publication in a tenth of the time it would have taken me. Without his zeal, it all might be a stack of papers, gathering dust, yellowing somewhere on the far side of my desk. But no. Over a weekend, he and his wife, Lisa, and my wife, Jan, and I did the proof-reading. Lisa and Jan have eagle-eyes for typos and are persnickety grammarians. I happily submitted to every suggestion.

Finally, the cover. Nancy Lindburg, an artist from Salem, Oregon, is, in herself, a replication of the beauty all around her. There is the beauty of her quick generosity, making this cover possible. Among the golden grain, there are the weeds. It's the story of life in the world — but we do have to take time to learn the difference and restrain ourselves until action is Godly. Think about that as you contemplate Nancy's painting (and read the sermon titled "Good Seed and Zizania").

Thank you for taking up this book. I hope you'll find good grain in it — and I hope you won't find weeds.

I pray you Christ's peace.

The Rt. Rev. John S. Thornton
Scio, Oregon
June 2016

The Unwisdom Of Solomon

By the luck of the Lectionary, I drew some stories from the Solomon cycle of stories in I Kings this morning.

Your parents read those Bible stories to you every night after supper when you were a kid or you read them when you took a Bible as Literature class in college or university. I'll make an effort to prevent you from sleeping through the repetition.

Everybody knows that Solomon was a wise man. The authors of I Kings won't let us forget. "And God gave Solomon wisdom and understanding exceeding much, and largeness of heart, even as the sand that is on the sea shore" (I Kings 4:29, KJV). "And there came of all people to hear the wisdom of Solomon, from all kings of the earth, which had heard of his wisdom" (I Kings 4:34, KJV).

First, I have to tell you – or remind you – how Solomon got to be king. Well, you say, he was the king's son, so why wouldn't he be next in line? It's not so simple when your dad is a polygamist. David had more wives and concubines than Scripture counts. So Solomon had a raft of half-brothers (and half-sisters too, though they're never mentioned, and there's no telling what happened to them.)

One of Solomon's half-brothers was Adonijah, the son of Haggith, one of David's many wives. (She was also Absolom's mother. You remember him.) According to the text, Adonijah was "a very handsome man." The King James Version says "goodly," which suggests a moral judgment, though he wasn't particularly goodly – or badly. It's just that Adonijah had this kingly feeling about himself; so he put together a committee to explore the feasibility of his becoming king. It consisted of Joab, the army's top general (whom David hated), and Abiathar, the high priest and a few others. They said, "Adonijah, you look like a king; so be a king." That was all there was to the feasibility study. He rounded up all his half-brothers, excepting, of course, Solomon, and the king's servants, excepting Nathan, the court prophet, and Zadok, a priest, and Benaiah and Shimei and Rei and all the other "mighty men" who were loyal to David. Adonijah's people sacrificed a lot of livestock and said many prayers, then crowned him King of Israel and had a big barbeque. Long live King Adonijah.

When David's people got wind of the crowning, they went straight to the person in power: the beautiful Bathsheba. Remember her? No one in the kingdom had as much leverage over David as she did. Frantically, they told her what Adonijah had done and that she had to talk with the King now. She marched right into the King's bedroom, and there he was, in bed with Abishag the Shunammite. Don't let your minds run wild now. Abishag was there to keep the dying man warm. And that's all. More about her later.

Bathsheba leaned over the terminal king and asked, "Didn't you say that our son Solomon would be king when you died?"

"Huh?"

"You did say that Solomon would be your successor, didn't you!"

"Uh-huh," David muttered.

Then Nathan and Benaiah and Shimei and Rei and the rest dashed into the bedroom to witness the declaration of succession.

Screwing up his last bit of energy, David told them to put Solomon on his mule and take him down to the Gishon and anoint him King. So they did, and they blew the ram's horn and summoned all Israel to come to the Gishon. "Long live King Solomon," they shouted. With oil running down his forehead and around his ears, he was the anointed one, the King.

When Adonijah's people heard the shouting, they were not pleased. It looked like it would be a short, hardly more than a barbecue-long, reign. It would be a short life for Adonijah, too. I'll tell you why.

Suddenly out of a job as king, Adonijah went to Bathsheba to ask for just one little favor. He thought he deserved some consolation for being so quickly and summarily deposed. All he wanted was Abishag the Shunammite for a wife. Remember her? She was the virgin who was recruited to keep David warm during his dying days (and, therefore, a concubine). That Abishag was so good-looking she could stop a camel train. (That's a very loose translation of the Hebrew.) So Bathsheba went to Solomon to ask if Adonijah could have Abishag the Shunammite for a wife. Solomon replied, acidly, "He wants what? Why doesn't he just ask for the whole kingdom?!" Back in those days, if you could wed the king's widow, you could get the kingdom too. Marriage to sweet Abishag would make Adonijah a rival to the throne. He and his supporters would have to be eliminated. Politics has always been a blood sport.

3

So "wise" Solomon – translate that "ruthless" – had Brother Adonijah bumped off. To avenge both his dad and himself, he had General Joab bumped off too. He was about to do the same thing to High Priest Abiathar, but then thought better of it. Even in ancient times, there was the ridiculous notion that when you're dealing with the clergy you're dealing with God. So he just fired Abiathar and told him to get out of town and stay out of town and die out of town and make it quick.

In spite of all the executions and banishments, today's lesson from I Kings establishes Solomon's reputation as a wise man.

While at Gibeon, Solomon was doing what he shouldn't have been doing, namely offering sacrifice and burning incense at a "high place." A "high place" was a place where the god Baal was worshiped. (See Psalm 121: "I will lift up mine eyes unto the hills, from whence cometh my help." The NRSV gets it right. It's a question. Where does my help come from? Well, it doesn't come from up there. "My help comes from the Lord, who made heaven and earth.") Anyway, while he was up there, Solomon had a dream in which the Lord God asked him what he wanted. Now this is tender. "O Lord, my God...I am but a little child. I do not know how to go out or come in." In other words, he didn't know which way was up. Actually, he was a "little child" only in the dream. Josephus, the Jewish historian, speculated that he was a teenager, already a king at the time. Whether a little child or a teenager, there was some kind of spiritual precocity going on in the young man. Just give me "an understanding mind," so that I'll know the difference between good and evil and will govern my people wisely. In the King James Version, he asks for "an understanding heart," which I like better, since the mind and the heart aren't the same thing. The Lord God – in the dream – says, "Because you didn't ask for riches or the death of your enemies, I'll give you what you ask and I'll give it to you in spades. However, you have to keep covenant with me or the deal's off. Did you hear me? You have to keep covenant with me or the deal's off. Do I have to say it again?" That's not a direct quote, but it's the substance of what the Lord God said in the dream.

I must say that the dream is slightly disingenuous. Solomon didn't have to pray for riches. He was already rich. He was born into riches. He was the richest kid in Israel. He drove around town in a Ferrari chariot drawn by two matching white stallions. The Bible doesn't say that. I'm just making it up, so that you won't lose interest and fall asleep. As for his enemies, his dad, David, had already killed them all, with the exception of those whom I've already mentioned.

The second story is even more famous than the first. It's the one about dividing the baby. It's in your bulletin. Take it home and read it. We're short on time.

There are lots of legends about the wisdom of Solomon. He *was* legendary. But the Solomon cycle of stories ends with the unwisdom, indeed the stupidity of the King of Israel.

Chapter 11, Verse 1: "But King Solomon loved many strange women (King James Version). The New Revised Standard Version has a better translation: "Now King Solomon loved many foreign women, the daughter of Pharaoh and Moabite, Ammonite, Edomite, Sidonian and Hittite women." Did he! He had seven hundred wives and three hundred concubines, it says. That's a thousand women! And that's an extreme case of OCD. He hoarded women. I'm so weak-minded – or testosterone-deprived – that I can't even imagine it. I have one wife, and there's not one in a thousand who could be better.

The trouble was that each of the non-Jewish wives and concubines came with her own gods and idols. Love me, love my god. Solomon became an unhinged, slaphappy polytheist. He loved Ashtoreth, the abomination of the Sidonians, and Milcom, the abomination of the Ammonites, and Chemosh, the abomination of the Moabites and Molech – oh, oh, Molech, the monstrous idol to whom those ancients sacrificed children. You say, those ancients were so primitive and ignorant and superstitious, but we are so sophisticated. Really? It's just as C.S. Lewis said, "We worship Christ but serve Molech." Our version of Molech is called The Gun, to which we sacrifice up to ten thousand children in America every year. Then there are wars, endless wars, in which children are disproportionately the casualties. Molech, such an idol he.

Scripture makes it very clear that the Lord God was not happy with Solomon…was angry…was furious…was wrathful…was going to make him take the consequences of his unfaithfulness. That's when the kingdom began to fall apart. Following Solomon, there wasn't a decent king, excepting Josiah, until the Babylonian Exile.

So why have I taken so much time with these Solomon stories? For the very same reason the authors of I Kings did. Not keeping covenant has consequences: division…decline…dire, dreadful, disastrous even. It happens when people do not love the Lord above all loves.

We Episcopalians have a covenant (and a Catechism) to order our lives with a great loyalty and to limit our actions to that which creates and redeems. Page 304, *The Book of Common Prayer.* We recite it whenever there's a baptism. We recite it whenever Bishop Michael comes. We recite it whenever Mother Anne, the chief liturgist in this church, thinks we should. Word for word, it's in our hearts.

"Will you proclaim by word and example the Good News of God in Christ?"

Yes, yes, yes, a thousand times yes.

"Will you seek and serve Christ in all persons, loving your neighbor as yourself?"

Absolutely. You can count on us.

"Will you strive for justice and peace among all people and respect the dignity of every human being?"

You can bet your life we will.

In the First Century, the Jesus People began the movement toward the radical equality of persons. "In Christ, there is neither Jew nor Greek, neither male nor female, neither slave nor free." Forget Aristotle's *Politics.* Forget Plato's *Republic.* Forget the whole hierarchy of human types in the ancient world in which only a few persons possessed true dignity. Those Jesus People asked the most urgent question of every era of history: Will we act as though every person is made in the image of God?

Jan and I just attended four days of the ten-day General Convention in Salt Lake City. It was "Pentecostal," as thrilling, I'll bet, as the original Pentecost in Jerusalem. There were thousands of us, six, seven, eight, nine, enough to fill the Salt Palace Convention Center. There were African Americans and Hispanic Americans and Asian Americans and American Indians and white folks like us, young, old, gay, straight, some in jogging clothes, some in wheelchairs, and, politically, some conservative and some liberal, some rich maybe, some poor maybe, all knowing that, without the love of Christ, our humanity is abjectly impoverished. If a coldhearted atheist had walked through the Convention as we worshiped, he would surely have remarked, "There's a peace and joy here that I don't feel anywhere else in the world." It's just as Pierre Teilhard de Chardin said, "The love of Christ is the only thing in the world that can make us one without destroying our differences." The General Convention was proof.

Here, at the altar of St. Paul's Church, it all begins. Here, as we're on our knees, on the same level, leveled and leveling, eating from the same loaf and drinking from the same cup, we become more and more like the Jesus People of the First Century. You may glance at the forgiven sinner on your left or on your right and wonder, "What's he (or she) doing here?" I assure you that she (or he) is wondering the same thing about you. So let me tell you what you're both doing there. In the sacrament, you're there to transcend your inhibitions and fears to love and to learn to embrace the other in his or her otherness, whether sweet or bewildering, as though you were embracing the sweet and bewildering Christ. Because of you, the world is changing.

My loves, we have a covenant to keep. It's not hard work; it's sacred play. So let's do it boldly and fearlessly and hilariously. Let the whole city know that the kingdom of heaven is breaking in at St. Paul's Church.

The Rt. Rev. John S. Thornton
St. Paul's Episcopal Church
Salem, Oregon
August 16, 2015

The Normal Christian

Let me get this chronology straight. Jesus, still dripping from his immersion in the water of the Jordan River – and immersed in the sensation that he was beloved of God – went into the wilderness, to fast, to pray, to make sure that he knew who he was *and* who he was not. He knew that, in this world, there's always the choice between serving God or serving "Satan." It's as stark as that. You either love or you don't.

Still weak from the battle within himself, having won clarity for his soul and a singular purpose, he began his work, as a kind of itinerant rabbi, teacher, healer, and exorcist – and "a friend of outcasts and sinners."

From town to town in lower Galilee he went, to Acco and Sephoris and Tiberius and Magdala and Capernaum he went. It was going well, in every village and synagogue. "He was praised by everyone," it says in today's Gospel (Luke 4:14). They loved him, and he loved them back. Or, more precisely, he loved them and they loved *him* back. However, he must have felt as if he were back in the wilderness again, having to own or sell himself. Serve God with humility or serve "Satan" with vainglory, those were the choices, every moment of every day. Humbly, he went on to other villages and synagogues.

Finally, he headed home, to Nazareth. It would be different. He knew it would be different – but he didn't know just how different it would be.

It's an old story. Plutarch said, "You will find that few of the most prudent and wise of mankind have been appreciated in their own country." And there's that proverb that often comes up in rabbinical writings: "Physician, heal thine own lameness." And this one: "In a sad state is the city whose physician has the gout and whose steward has one eye." Typically, we take a person's defects or impairments or moral failures – anything that will allow us to make him/her inferior and, by comparison, ourselves superior – and construct a whole personality around those things. Then, we relate, not to the real person, but to the personality we've constructed.

On the Sabbath Day, Jesus went to the synagogue, "as his custom was," it says. Whether it was his turn or he volunteered or he was called on to read, we'll never know. All it says is that "he stood up to read."

(This isn't important for you to know, but "he stood up to read" isn't an idle comment. In the synagogues, the reader stood to read from Torah and the Major Prophets, but not from the Minor Prophets. In other words, from Isaiah, but not, say, from Micah.)

The *hazzan* (attendant) handed him the scroll of the Prophet Isaiah. He unrolled it to, in our Bibles, Chapter 61. There were not chapters and verses back in those days. It's the soliloquy of what we used to call the "Righteous Servant of Jehovah" or, simply, a "Servant Song." I read from the King James Version, which I prefer, not that the NRSV isn't a good translation.

"The Spirit of the Lord is upon me;
because the Lord hath anointed me to preach good tidings
unto the poor;
he hath sent me to bind up the brokenhearted,
to proclaim liberty to the captives
and the opening of the prison to them that are bound;
to proclaim the acceptable year of the Lord,
and the day of vengeance of our God;
to comfort all who mourn."

You can imagine that some of the people were saying, "Oh, what a beautiful lesson." Some others were saying, "Oh, he reads so well." Some, I'd guess, were saying, "Oh, we're so glad he's home again."

He rolled up the scroll and handed it back to the *hazzon* and sat down. Then he quickly stood up again and looked them all straight in the eye and said, "Today, this scripture has been fulfilled in your hearing."

"What?"

"Fulfilled?"

"In you?"

"Just who do you think you are?"

"We know your dad."

"You must think you're God Almighty!"

"How arrogant!"

"No, it's worse than that. It's blasphemous!!!"

They grew more agitated and crazed, as religious people do when someone points out to them that their religion is religion, not the love of God above all loves. My religion hasn't gotten me to the verge of heaven; it has gotten me to the edge of hell, they may, one day, realize.

Feeling murderously righteous, the men of the synagogue marched Jesus off to "the place of execution." However, because Palestine was under Roman rule, the synagogue's "bench of three" didn't have the power to condemn Jesus to death. They settled for what was called "a rebel's beating": cursing, spitting, punching, kicking, over and over again, a beating that was meant to make Jesus repent of any notion that he could possibly be the Righteous Servant of Jehovah or anyone like him. Bruised and bleeding, he managed to get away, a prophet everywhere but in his own hometown.

That's what happens when, in a religious system, anybody's religious system, people are indoctrinated and catechized and drilled to assume that God is "up there," not down here; that God is beyond, not within; that there is no such thing as the humanity of God.

The Gospel is that Jesus of Nazareth is "God with us," in person. And what was true of Jesus is true – or certainly can be – of us.

We tend – or even prefer – to believe that Jesus was totally different from us. We like to think that he was super-human, so that we don't have to strive for his likeness and, besides, even the striving wouldn't do it. The Church Fathers were very clear about that misunderstanding: "(He) was tempted in every way as we are, but did not sin." Or, as we say in the Consecration Prayer, "(He) lived and died as one of us." Jesus was clear about it too, often abruptly and gruffly.

Once, they tried to talk him into being their king, but he would have no part of it. "My kingdom is not of this world."

Once, two young men who were fighting over their inheritance approached him. They addressed him, obsequiously, as "good teacher." He snapped, "No one is good, but God alone."

Once, unequivocally, he said, "You think I do great things, but you can do greater things than these."

When Jesus read from Isaiah in the synagogue in Nazareth and said that the Scripture was fulfilled, he was talking not only about himself but also about everyone there. The "Servant Song" was meant to be a description of all Jews and, now, all Christians too. It is normal for Jews and Christians to think and act like the "Righteous Servant of Jehovah."

The norm for Christians is to bring good news to the poor, of whom there are millions in America, some of them right here, maybe next door, since poverty takes many forms.

The norm for Christians is to bind up the brokenhearted, in our families, among our friends and acquaintances, in anyone whose eyes bespeak sorrow or defeat.

The norm for Christians is to liberate the captives, all who are captivated in ways that take away their freedom and destroy their lives.

The norm for Christians is to open the prisons to them that are bound, particularly those who have been imprisoned for crimes they did not commit or for non-violent crimes, in this country that incarcerates a greater percentage of its citizens than any country in the world.

The norm for Christians is to proclaim the acceptable year of the Lord, the year, to a day, of a prevalent and systemic mercy.

The norm for Christians is to proclaim the day of vengeance of our God. Oops! Vengeance? I remind you of an unbalanced and un-redemptive Christianity with the words of H. Richard Niebuhr: "A God without wrath brought men without sin into a Kingdom without judgment through the ministrations of a Christ without a Cross." Our unlove has immediate and vengeful ("wrathful") consequences and those consequences may last for generations.

The norm for Christians is to comfort all who mourn. "Blessed are those who mourn," the Beatitude goes. Comforting those who mourn is how you know that you have the capacity for empathy, so still alive and very human.

The norm for Christians is to live as Jesus lived, to believe and to act as though

"The Spirit of the Lord is upon me;
because he hath anointed me to preach good tidings to the poor;
he hath sent me to bind up the brokenhearted,
to proclaim liberty to the captives,
and the opening of the prison to those that are bound;
to proclaim the acceptable year of the Lord,
and the day of vengeance of our God;
to comfort all that mourn."

That, Jesus showed us, is how the Divine becomes human, normally.

The Rt. Rev. John S. Thornton
St. Thomas Episcopal Church
Eugene, Oregon
January 6, 2016

Love Is The Way

Forget the Virgin Birth. You heard me. Forget it. I'm not saying that the doctrine isn't useful; it is, very. However, it gets to be a huge distraction. It's never mentioned in Paul's epistles, the oldest documents we have. And the oldest gospel, Mark, on which both Matthew and Luke depend, makes no reference to it. For Luke, Joseph and Mary are betrothed, married or about to be married, and Mary is pregnant. Unless you want to fight over the Greek word that we usually translate "betrothed," that's it for Luke. It isn't important, except to prudes and professors. For Matthew though, it's a miraculous conception and a "how-could-that-be?" puzzlement for the ages – and, of course, endless and boring debates. John, the writer of the Fourth Gospel, was too busy writing about universal and eternal things to refer to it, if there was anything to refer to. Of course, it's in the Nicene Creed, which we recite every Sunday. The problem is that we American Christians have always been cursed by the notion that everything in the Bible should be literally true. Really, I want you to forget about the Virgin Birth. For now, ALL YOU NEED TO KNOW IS THAT MARY HAD A BABY.

I know, you can't forget about it. You want to know who the biological father of Jesus was. It's beyond Paul, or Paul is beyond it. Mark isn't interested in parentage; he's interested in the Messiahship of Jesus. Luke seems pretty clear about it: it was Joseph. There's no hint of illegitimacy. But Matthew thinks there's something funny (the scholarly term is "irregular") about Mary's pregnancy. Hmmm. John has no interest in biology; he's interested in theology. (Emphatically, however, John says that "the Word became flesh," that the Spirit takes a body and walks around and says and does things that are, as we say these days, "awesome.") There are other theories. Whether it's prurience or Puritanism that keeps us fascinated and fixated on this, we might as well give up. We'll never know. From the perspective of the Cross, it doesn't make any difference. For now, ALL WE NEED TO KNOW IS THAT MARY HAD A BABY.

Was Jesus born in Bethlehem? By now, you know that Paul was totally disinterested in the birthplace of Jesus. His interest is in the Risen Christ. Mark doesn't mention the birthplace either. He begins his gospel with the baptism of the thirty year-old Jesus. Luke says that the birthplace was Bethlehem. So does Matthew. John doesn't locate the birth of the man who can be located only in the heart of God. Some scholars doubt that Jesus could have been born in Bethlehem and say that the birthplace had to have been Joseph's and Mary's hometown, Nazareth. One ancient commentator says that Mary gave birth on the journey from Nazareth to Bethlehem, but nobody knows where. Try Jericho. For the fulfillment of Old Testament prophecies, it's necessary that the birthplace be Bethlehem, "the city of David." Ultimately, Bethlehem or Nazareth or somewhere in between is not anywhere near as important as Calvary, the location of the Grand Miracle, the forgiveness of those who didn't know what they were doing (and of us when we don't know what we're doing either). "Unawareness is the root of all evil," we used to say. For now, ALL YOU NEED TO KNOW IS THAT MARY HAD A BABY.

Was Jesus born on December 25th? No. December 25th is a contrivance. It dates from the Fourth Century, when Roman Christians celebrated "the Sun of Righteousness," to counteract the popularity of the pagan's celebration of "Natalis Solis Invicti" ("the birth of the invincible

Sun"). Besides, there weren't any shepherds out in the fields, "keeping watch over their flocks by night." It was freezing, and there wasn't any vegetation out there on those hills in the dead of winter. (I've been there in the winter.) Heavens, shepherds and their sheep were in town, trying to keep warm. They lived together, in the same houses. Scholars say that the birth of Jesus had to have taken place between March and November. Clement of Alexandria (circa 150 to circa 215 A.D.) came up with an exact date: May 20th. Others claimed it was April 21st. Only Mary and Joseph would have known, and they were long dead when the gospels were written and couldn't be interviewed. Furthermore, the date of the birth isn't critical. This is an eternal event. For now, ALL YOU NEED TO KNOW IS THAT MARY HAD A BABY.

Did Mary wrap her baby in "swaddling cloths"? I'll bet you anything that she did. Any Palestinian mother would have done that.

Did Mary lay her baby in a manger? Mothers did that all the time in those days. People and animals lived in the same houses, the animals on the lower level, the people on the upper. The mangers, in the floor itself, were on the upper level, so that the animals could stand and eat. When the animals slept, a manger was the perfect place to lay a baby.

Did an angel tell shepherds to leave their sheep and get over to see that child? Well, it seems fanciful; but I wasn't there to follow those ragged, reeking fellows around. They did have a tenderness toward newborns, as all shepherds do.

Look, this is the Twenty-First Century. Jesus was born twenty-one hundred years ago. All we have to go on is the Greek New Testament. We can pore over the text word by word and come up with right interpretations or wrong ones. Though it may seem anti-intellectual and insouciant, for now ALL YOU NEED TO KNOW IS THAT MARY HAD A BABY.

Mary had a baby and that baby become a boy and that boy became a man and those who encountered that man exclaimed:

That man's whole life is begotten of God!
That man's whole life is conceived of the Holy Spirit!
That man's whole life is born of the
One who is holy and righteous!
He's something else!!!

And so, apart from, even in spite of, many of the little details in those beautiful, unforgettable, absolutely theologically true Nativity stories, we believe that God sent His son to all His sons and daughters in the world crying, Love is the way! Even from the cross, the crude cross, the cruel cross, he could gasp the Word of God: Love is the way.

My loves, we won't be saved by our knowledge of Scripture or our knowledge of theology or our knowledge of Church history — or even by our church-going. We will be saved only by our acts of love. So our church-going has to be an act of love. And our worship has to be an act of love. And every decision we make every day about everything whatsoever has to be our way of saying, Love is the way.

Though some of my colleagues have suggested that there's something slightly "irregular" about my theology, I want you to know that they're wrong. I am not the least bit original. I am, in my mind, happily and hilariously, traditional and orthodox. To wit, my favorite prayer from the 1928 *Book of Common Prayer* is this: "O Lord, who hast taught us that all our doings without charity are nothing worth; Send thy Holy Ghost, and pour into our hearts that most excellent gift of charity, the very bond of peace and all virtues, without which whosoever liveth is counted dead before thee. Grant this for thine only Son, Jesus Christ's sake. Amen." If I had to choose one prayer from *The Book of Common Prayer,* that would be it.

With all my heart, I do believe that "all our doings without charity are nothing worth" and that without charity "whosoever liveth is counted dead before thee." Love is the way, the only way into the heart of the God. It's hate that kills us (and others). Unless we go love's way, we're contributing nothing to the lives of others - and, at the same time, nothing to our own – and nothing to the world for which our Lord, for love, gave his life. We're hardly more than dead.

Love is the way.
Go that way!
Never go any other way!
Go that way even if nobody else goes that way!
Never turn back!
Go, go, go Christ-ward!
And don't be afraid.

The Rt. Rev. John S. Thornton
St. Thomas Episcopal Church
Sun Valley, Idaho
December 27, 2015

In And Out Of The Lion's Den

I'm still in *The Book of Daniel. Daniel* is between Ezekiel and Hosea in the Hebrew Scriptures, just in case you haven't read it recently. This is my third sermon on *Daniel,* and there may be a fourth and a fifth. Who, other than God, knows? There's something forever contemporaneous and forever relevant about *Daniel.*

To recap: to cover up its subversiveness, *Daniel* pretends to be about events that occurred during the Fifth and Fourth Centuries B.C., during the Exile in Babylon. But *Daniel* is really about the conditions that existed in Palestine during the first quarter of the Second Century B.C., when Antiochus Epiphanes was the ruler. You remember, from previous sermons, that Antiochus called himself "Epiphanes," meaning "illustrious" or, even, "glorious" in Greek. Ever since he was a kid, he had an outsized ego and no superego at all. He turned out to be a sociopath with a crown on his head. For him, cruelty was, well, fun. He had zero capacity for empathy. Nobody dared tell him because, if he did, he'd be the object of Antiochus' cruelty. He saved his cruelty, as if there were any left to save, for the Jews in Palestine. He did everything he could to destroy Judaism, such as turning the Temple into a shrine to Zeus Olympus and ordering the sacrifice of pigs. Pigs!? The animals the Jews hated the most. And on and on. He would live and die without ever knowing how evil he was. That's why the Jews nicknamed him "Antiochus Epimanes." "Epimanes" is Greek for "nincompoop," which was, absolutely, the nicest thing that could ever be said about him. "Madman" or "monster" comes closer.

The Book of Daniel was meant to be an encouragement to the Jews who lived during the reign of Antiochus Epiphanes. Your present condition won't be your permanent condition. Take heart! Have faith in the God of your fathers! Antiochus Epimanes will get his just desserts! God's kingdom will never be destroyed! You'll see! Believe me, you'll see.

As the sixth chapter of *Daniel* begins, Darius the Mede is the King in Babylon. Nebuchadnezzar is dead. His successor, Belshazzar, is dead too. Kings have their armies, but their armies can't protect them against the Angel of Death.

Darius I (522-486 B.C.) was a genius at organization. He set up a system of a hundred and twenty satrapies, of which a satrap (or governor) was in charge. It would be like having a satrap of Idaho and a satrap of Oregon and a satrap of Wyoming and so on. Over all one hundred and twenty satraps (governors) there were three presidents. You don't need to know all this, except that *Daniel* was one of those three presidents. He had organizational and communications skills such as no one had ever seen...and energy...and charm...and everything. The King was about to make him the president of the presidents. Oops! The other presidents and some of the satraps started talking. You know, he's from Palestine. You know, he's a Jew. You know, those people stick together and they stick with their God, whatever they call him. It was all because of jealousy. Jealousy. Insane jealousy.

May I remind you that jealousy, though it isn't, officially, one of the "deadly sins," sure can be lethal. It's going to cause destruction. It could be your own. It could, of course, destroy your integrity and your friendships and your reputation and, long after you're dead, the memory of you. Jealousy just reinforces your sense of inferiority. The way for you to feel superior is for the person who actually is superior to be put down – or put away, canned summarily – or, back in those days, merrily mauled and munched by starving lions, hee, hee.

So this little party of conspirators, under the pretense of loyalty to king and country, marched off to see the King, with a proposal. "O King Darius, may you live forever!" That greeting makes a king as giddy as "My Lord" makes a bishop. With all these exiles and immigrants and freethinkers around, what this kingdom needs is a loyalty oath. We have to have some unity or there will be all kinds of un-Persian activities going on. They didn't mean unity; they meant uniformity. They meant control. They meant subjugation. It would be like the McCarthy era in the U.S. or the closed primary in Idaho or a church that bullies people into believing doctrines and dogmas that have little or nothing to do with the essence of Christianity or the progress of humankind. Make things narrower and narrower, until the very life of the God of Love is squeezed out. The King, still giddy from that "may you live forever!" greeting didn't catch on to their real motive. There must be, the schemers said, an interdict "that whoever prays to anyone, divine or human, for thirty days, except to you, O King, shall be thrown into a den of lions." Good idea, the King said. Show me where to sign. They'd built a trap for Daniel, hee, hee. They'd built one for the king too.

Daniel knew all about the interdict. He didn't care what it said. Though he was happy to serve the King and the kingdom, his greater loyalty was to the God of Abraham and Isaac and Jacob, to the Creator of heaven and earth. So, three times a day, he looked toward

Jerusalem and got down on his knees and prayed for "mercy" for all the peoples in Persia. The plotters knew he did that and, of course, they ratted on him. "O King Darius, may you live forever!" You signed the interdict which, for the love of this land, we brought to you; but your man Daniel continues to violate it. Three times a day he prays to his God. He deserves to die.

That's when the King realized that, along with Daniel, he'd been trapped. For the life of his best president, he tried everything he could to save him; but the schemers kept harassing him with, The law's the law. If you don't keep it, nobody has to keep it. Be a king, King. Daniel has to die. And the King went into a funk, partly because he'd been such a fool, and a damned one too.

The King had no choice but to order that Daniel be thrown into the den of starving lions. His last words to Daniel were, "May your God, whom you faithfully serve, deliver you!" Then the King went to his palace and fasted and prayed through the night, without a wink of sleep.

At dawn, the King went to the lions' den – and there was Daniel, alive, cuddled up with the lions as if they were pussycats. Not a bite. Not a scratch. Nothing. Nothing but a scene like "The Peaceable Kingdom." Daniel explained that an angel of the Lord had caused the lions to have lockjaw and weak knees – because God knew that Daniel had done no wrong.

The King was relieved and exuberant – and mad, outraged and furious. His own people had tricked him. So…he commanded that they and their wives and their children, all of them, be thrown into the den of lions. It was not pretty. Scripture says "the lions over-powered them and broke all their bones in pieces." (I remind you that this is an allegory. Who knows how much, if any of it, might be historical?)

The story has a happy ending. King Darius wrote to all the people in the world, it says, in their own languages, it says: "I make a decree, that…people should tremble and fear before the God of Daniel.

For his is the living God,
  Enduring forever.
His kingdom shall never be destroyed,
  And his dominion has no end.
He delivers and rescues,
  He works signs and wonders
  In heaven and on earth…"

Do you believe that? Do you believe that God's kingdom will never be destroyed? Do you believe that God's dominion has no end? Do you believe that God delivers and rescues? Do you believe that God works signs and wonders in heaven and on earth? If not, your life will run down to pessimism and negativity and hopelessness and alienation and dark, dark gloom. The world's never going to change, you'll say. People are never going to change. All of which means, I'm never going to change either. As Martin Buber said, "Nothing can doom man more than the belief in doom." But if you do believe it, you'll see signs and wonders everywhere. "Holy, holy, holy, Lord God of hosts, heaven and earth are full of your glory," will be your song. Then you yourself will be a sign and a wonder, fully alive,

God "contracted" (Nicholas of Cusa) in you. And you'll be the person who'll help others understand that God's kingdom will never be destroyed, that God's dominion has no end. That's what our Lord helped people to understand. "The kingdom of God is in the midst of us," he said again and again. We're in the midst of it. Because of the way you love your life and love the lives of others and love this earth that sustains us all, people will know that what can be imagined can also be real every day. Shalom.

The Rt. Rev. John S. Thornton
St. Michael's Cathedral
Boise, Idaho
June 29, 2014

Ruth

Today's Old Testament lesson is from *The Book of Ruth*. You know, *Genesis, Exodus, Leviticus, Numbers, Deuteronomy, Joshua, Judges, Ruth.* It's a love story, one of the best ever. It's a short book, only four chapters long.

There was a famine in Judah. A Bethlehemite family, Elimelech and his wife, Naomi, and their two sons, Mahlon and Chilion, go down to Moab, across the Jordan, in hope of survival. (I must tell you that "Mahlon," in Hebrew, means "sickly," and, in Hebrew, "Chilion" means "wasting away." Those kids were in bad shape.) After a few years, Elimelech died, leaving a wife and two sons to make it on their own. Evidently, they did. Mahlon and Chilion got through childhood and youth and married Moabite women, Mahlon to Ruth and Chilion to Orpah. Not long into those marriages, both Mahlon and Chilion died, leaving two young widows, Ruth and Orpah. No children. Neither had a means of support.

Naomi told her daughters-in-law to stay right there in Moab and find husbands. She was going back to Bethlehem where, at least, she had a parcel of land and some relatives and friends. Orpah, after protesting, decided to stay. Ruth, who loved her mother-in-law more than anyone on earth, didn't think twice about it. She'd go with her, to a strange land.

Ruth's speech to Naomi is some of the most beautiful language in the Bible:

"Intreat me not to leave thee,
or to return from following after thee:
for whither thou goest, I will go;
and where thou lodgest, I will lodge:
thy people shall be my people,
and thy God my God:
Where thou diest, will I die,
and there will I be buried:
the Lord do so to me, and more also,
if ought but death part thee and me."

Off they went to Bethlehem, just in time for the barley harvest. To survive, Ruth became a gleaner, picking up whatever the reapers missed or dropped. She worked all day, from dawn to dusk, without a break. The owner of the field where Ruth was gleaning, a man named Boaz (who, as it turned out, was one of Elimelech's "kinsmen") noticed her, not only because she was so hardworking, but also because she was so pretty. He asked the boss of the reapers, "Who's that young woman over there?"

"Oh, that's Naomi's daughter-in-law, the young widow from Moab."

"Really!"

Boaz took Ruth aside and told her not to glean in any other field. He'd see to it that she was protected. Among the young reapers, she wouldn't be safe. But, said Ruth, "Why do this for me? I'm a foreigner."

"I've heard what you've done for Naomi. May the Lord repay you as much – and more," said Boaz.

They had lunch together, bread and wine, a kind of eucharist. Boaz, obviously, was smitten.

At the end of the day, Ruth told Naomi about the man whose field she had been gleaning. "Blessed be the Lord!" Naomi shouted. "He's a relative! And he's rich! And he'd be next in line to marry you!" (In fact, Boaz wasn't first in line; he was second in line. We'll get to that in a minute.)

Ruth gleaned through the barley harvest and through the wheat harvest, never slackened, never complained, just got prettier and prettier in the eyes of Boaz. He was ripe for the harvest. Naomi knew. "I need to get you married – but not just to anybody. To Boaz. Here's how you'll do it. You bathe and get into your best clothes and, at the end of the day, go down to Boaz' threshing floor, but not before he has eaten and drunk some wine and is slightly daffy and defenseless. Notice where he lies down for the night, then go over and uncover his feet and lie down. Then do whatever he tells you to do."

At midnight, Boaz, sensing someone's presence, sat bolt upright. There was a person lying at his feet. "Who's that?"

"It's Ruth, Naomi's daughter-in-law, the gleaner. Spread your skirt over me."

Now don't get any ideas. It wasn't sex; it was symbolism. Ruth, in effect, was saying, "Take me under your protection. If you want me, I'm all yours."

"Bless you. You could marry any number of young men, but you've chosen to marry me, an old man. But there's still a problem. I'm not really the next of kin. There's one other man. You leave while it's still dark, so that nobody sees us together. In the morning, I'll take care of this."

Off she went, brighter than the moon.

In the morning, Boaz went to the town gate, where the men met, to discuss business and weather and politics and to do transactions in the presence of witnesses. Elimelich's (Naomi's late husband's) next of kin showed up as usual. Boaz explained the situation to him: Naomi had to sell a parcel of land; and, since he was next of kin, he could redeem it or not.

"I'll redeem it," be blurted. "How much?"

"Not so fast," Boaz said. "If you buy the field from Naomi, you're also buying her daughter-in-law, Ruth the Moabite, the widow of the dead."

"Well," he said, "I can't do that. I'd mess up my whole inheritance. You can have my right of redemption."

He took off one sandal and gave it to Boaz, and Boaz took off one sandal and gave it to him. That's how transactions were "sealed" back in those days. Boaz had bought Naomi's field – and, better than that, Naomi's daughter-in-law. He had bought heaven on earth.

So Boaz and Ruth became husband and wife. It's wasn't long before they had a baby, named Obed. Cute kid, Obed. And nobody was happier than Naomi, who, finally, had her "security," a grandson.

At the very end of the Book of Ruth, there's a genealogy. It looks tacked on. It was tacked on. According to many scholars, it was tacked on for political purposes. When the Jews returned from exile in Babylon, Ezra and Nehemiah, the priests, ordered the men to divorce their foreign wives, to keep their religion from being defiled by strange gods. A large number of men had no intention of doing that. They loved their foreign wives. Why, God can use our foreign wives to further His plan of salvation just as much as he can use Jewish wives. Take Ruth for instance. Without her, we wouldn't have gotten Obed. Without Obed, we wouldn't have gotten Jesse. Without Jesse, we wouldn't have gotten David. King David! So get off your purification kick.

Matthew's Gospel begins with that very same genealogy and goes on from David to Joseph, "the husband of Mary, of whom Jesus was born." That genealogy contains the names of four Old Testament women: Rahab, Tamar, Ruth and "the wife of Uriah." That's Bathsheba, whose name they're hesitant to mention. So why those four?

Because they were all sinners, said Jerome (St. Jerome). He meant, of course, sexual sinners. He was busy translating the Hebrew and

Greek Scriptures into Latin, but he couldn't get sex off his mind. Oh well, it's the human condition. Rahab was a prostitute; Tamar was a seductress; Ruth was – well, we'll never know what happened that night; and Bathsheba was an adulteress. Bad – or just compromised – as they might have been, they could never have frustrated God's grace and power. No human being can do that.

Martin Luther thought those four women were included because they were all foreigners. Rahab and Tamar were Canaanites, Ruth was a Moabite and, Bathsheba, most likely, was a Hittite. So get over it, xenophobes. God can accomplish His purpose through foreigners if He wants to. He's the Creator of heaven and earth and knows no borders.

Many scholars, including Raymond Brown, say that the four women were chosen because there was, to put it nicely, something "irregular" in their histories. Matthew seems to want us to know that there was something slightly "irregular" in Mary's relationship with Joseph. But, ultimately, it doesn't make any difference. It doesn't invalidate God's action. Through those two, Mary and Joseph, God sent His Son into the world to cry, "Love is the Way." Even from the Cross, he cried, "Love is the Way."

There's something slightly "irregular" in all our histories. They call us broken, and we are; but we're not broken beyond our usefulness. We don't condition God; God conditions us. If God wants to redeem the world through us, He can jolly well do it. And that is what He wants to do through us. So why not go along with it as joyfully as Ruth? Love is the Way.

The Rt. Rev. John S. Thornton
St. Bede's Episcopal Church
Forest Grove, Oregon
November 8, 2015

Stuart And Lisa
At The Blessing Of Their Covenant

"There's a sweet, sweet Spirit in this place,
And I know that it's the Spirit of the Lord;
There are sweet expressions on each face,
And I know they feel the presence of the Lord."

Lisa, Stuart isn't the only man in the world. And yet he is the only man in the world which, by love and for love, you and he have created.

Stuart, Lisa isn't the only woman in the world. And yet she is the only woman in the world which, by love and for love, you and she have created.

This can be your Eden of renewal and gratefulness and wonder and delight and an unfathomable peace. Tend it.

Stuart, I remember your excitement, your giddiness and glee, when you told me that you had found the woman you had looked for all your life. It was with the intermediacy of the Internet. Old Luddite that I am, I asked myself, Can any good come out of *that* Nazareth? Was this marriage made in heaven or was it made in cyberspace? But, when you took me to meet her, over breakfast at Café de Paris, I took one look at Lisa and said, Wow! This darned thing works! I knew right away that, not only had you found the woman you have been looking for all your life, you had found yourself in her. A few bites later, I knew that she had found herself in you too. I can't remember what we had for breakfast, but everything had the taste of all that's right and all that's good, with all the sweetness of them.

I said that you two had found yourselves in each other. It's the work – no, it's the play – of the unconscious, which always takes your side. (Your unconscious knows when you can give yourself away.) Though you're both smart, it's the play of Someone – that's "Someone" with a capital "S" – who's a whole lot smarter than either of you or both of you together. I'm talking about the Spirit of God. The Church is right to call it "the mystery of love." And it's not only the above-quoted mystery; it's a miracle. Every act of love is miraculous. Though some scientists might like to, it's can't be reduced to something neurobiological, as if we were only a human animal. It's God's acting in us, exceeding the limits we've set for ourselves – or our societies and cultures have set for us – and revealing our capacity for everything from empathy to sacrifice.

Speaking of mysteries, Lisa, in the beginning Stuart was a mystery, though you felt safe in it. (That unconscious again.) As the days and weeks went by, he became less and less so, until, now, he's literally an open book. You've read it, *SOUTHERN FRIED FICTION.* My God! I've read the book too, from the manuscript state on. Two-thirds of the people in this congregation have read the book. (If you are in the one-third who haven't read it, Google Amazon immediately following the reception.) He's not hiding anything. Few among the people I know are so willing to risk that much transparency – and other people's judgments, not to mention other people's envy. You know what you're getting, Lisa, and what you're getting is an unusually brave man.

You two, as I said, have created a world, and that world can be Edenic. However, human relations can be perfected only to a degree, though often to a degree suggesting perfection. Still, there's one ego per person on the planet; and when two persons meet, there can be calamity or there can be communion. I've listened to you and I've watched you closely for months now, and I believe that you've become what those ancient psychologists and theologians called "one flesh," that's one heart and one soul and one in bed and one at table.

My daughter once asked me if my wife ever annoys me. "She does," I said, "but not often, and she never intends to. But it doesn't make any difference anyway. When you're loved as much as I'm loved, you love any annoyance." Put it all in perspective. What I know about the divine love I've learned from my wife, by extrapolation. My prayer is that you, Stuart, will learn as much from Lisa and that you, Lisa, will learn as much from Stuart. The Word becomes flesh and eats with you and sleeps with you and, in the cool of the day, walks through Eden with you.

Sometimes, when the two of you are ushers at a Sunday morning service and I am at the altar, I can see you back there, in the Narthex. Everybody who's coming to church has come, and everybody is focused on lectern or pulpit or altar or the figure of the Christ in stained glass above the altar. Nobody is looking back. But I can see you back there, in the half-light, holding hands – and embracing – in the House of God. I can see you. And I say to myself, Oh, God, look at those two. Look at them! How beautiful it is that they are so free to love – even in the middle of the Prayer of Consecration. *Eros* (romantic love) and *agape* (holy love) are not mutually exclusive. I plead with you: Keep it up. Never get tired of romance. Set other people free to love in the warring world. Time's wasting.

You're entering into a lifelong covenant here at St. Michael's Cathedral. You could have gone to a park or rented a hall or gathered your friends at a winery or gone up in a hot air balloon with a preacher who might have enough hot air to keep the balloon ascending. You're here because this has become the house of your hearts. This is the place where you've received so much grace and where parishioners have so readily and gratefully received your grace. It just has to be here, where there has been so much laughter and so many tears and always that high, high hope of our lives becoming more and more like the life of Christ. It just has to be here, where we all have such an intense feeling of the terrible tenderness of the Holy God.

So, Lisa and Stuart, you've created a world and you've invited us into it. On behalf of everybody here and many more, I thank you. And, furthermore, you've invited the Risen Christ into your world, to be your companion and to be your guide and, with his boundaryless and antic empathy and his mischievous mercy, to be your judge. Take each other's hand – take His too. Go. Go confidently and courageously into and through this world – and punctuate your joy with many victories at Bocce Ball.

"There's a sweet, sweet Spirit in this place,
And I know that it's the Spirit of the Lord;
There are sweet expressions on each face,
And I know they feel the presence of the Lord."

The Rt. Rev. John S. Thornton
St. Michael's Cathedral
Boise, Idaho
July 11, 2015

David And Brian, In Covenant

"Intreat me not to leave thee," she said to her. "Or to return from following after thee," she said to her. "For wither thou goest, I will go," she said to her. "Where thou lodgest, I will lodge," she said to her. "Where thou diest, I will die," she, Ruth, said to her, Naomi. Ruth to Naomi, woman to woman. It was daughter-in-law to mother-in-law, but who would quibble when two hearts are one? Those words in *The Book of Ruth* have, since ancient times, seemed the utterance of the Divine. They seem so still; and not a whisper, but a shout. "Intreat me not to leave thee," either spouse or God.

Whenever two people, two women, two men, say David Williams and Brian Judd, enter into a relationship of unlimited liability for a lifetime, we should fall on our knees and repent of every snide or snarky or simply bigoted thing we've ever thought or said about same-sex marriage. Pray for the undoing of all that.

Whenever two people, two women, two men, these two right here – just as Aelred of Rievaux, the Twelfth Century monk of Yorkshire, said – "wish to become one instead of two, since he (or she) is the one to whom you entrust yourself, from whom you hide nothing, from whom you fear nothing," that's when we should fall on our knees and beg for such grace as would bind us, soul to soul, with those sent into our lives, beginning with those who dwell under our roof and all who dwell under the roof of heaven. Take part in this gleeful, God-ward evolution.

Whenever two people, two women, two men, the two before us now, are compelled to dare an uncommon love and – I'm remembering two lines from a Shakespeare sonnet: "Love alters not with his brief hours and weeks, but bears it out even to the edge of doom." – and promise, swear, vow "for better for worse, for richer for poorer, in sickness and in health" even to "the edge of doom," that's when we should fall on our knees – no, stand up, up – to honor the magnanimity of lowliness, of no longer I alone, but we together. Is that not a realization of the Gospel? Greater love hath no one.

Oh, my loves, we've been so obsessed with sex that we've been blind to what's noble. Today, we, once blind, see.

Suddenly, we've gotten smarter. Diversity increases intelligence, they've found. It increases understanding. It increases empathy. It increases freedom. It increases community and, within it, the potential, the probability, of communion. It increases peace. It increases the "size" of God – God, who, so we see, is large enough to embrace us all, God who is so insinuative, so impartial, so mischievous as to appear in any of us at any time. Because of the increase hailed in this moment, I can no longer live in a constantly shrinking universe, until it consists only of me, of my gender, of my religion, of my politics, of my "truth" (a cobbling of half-truths and falsehoods), all boundaries and borders against surpassing astonishment, all against everything that's more than middling and mediocre, all against the lightheartedness and hilarity of living in this beautiful world with all these beautiful people.

Have you ever noticed – or, having noticed, made it an article of your creed – that we're not in control of either Nature or the Spirit of God? If not, Nicodemus and all in his likeness, loosen up. Like the wind, the Spirit "blows where it wills." So now we know that there are more than two ways to be human, contrary to what, Bible in hand, they told us and taught us (and tyrannized us). So now we know that there's more than one way to form a family. So now we know that, if we're going to be truly human and carefreely incarnate in this wide, wonderful, often whacky, often – oh, God help us – warring world, our hourly spiritual task is the perfection of love.

David and Brian, brave ones, guide us.

Today, Brian and David, is the anniversary of your legal marriage. Today, you sacralize your lifelong covenant with each other. Today, we enter into a covenant of friendship with you. So…intreat us not to leave thee…or to return from following after thee…for whither thou goest, we will go…and where thou lodgest, we will lodge…thy people shall be our people, and thy God our God. We swear it.

The Rt. Rev. John S. Thornton
St. Michael's Cathedral
Boise, Idaho
February 29, 2016

Erik H. Erikson

"We will remember
Always remember
We will remember"

I've been blessed as few people have been blessed. Erik Erikson and I became friends. Except for the fact that we were in the same place at the same time, I'll never know why. Beyond explanation, we just liked each other; and our liking grew into the suggestion, into the possibility, of a love "how deep, how broad, how high, how passing thought and fantasy."

Back in the '70s, I spent a lot of time at the home of Erik and Joan Erikson on Centro West, in Tiburon, California. Since I was the parish priest, I didn't need an excuse for that first call. But I made excuses for the next dozen or so calls. Then it became routine, like saying my prayers. My conversation with God and my conversation with the Eriksons seemed equally urgent to me. Now I know that I just needed to be with them, to learn how to become human. They were so astonishingly tolerant of that need, so astonishingly welcoming every time I knocked on their door (sometimes quite early in the morning, sometimes late in the afternoon, often at lunchtime), so astonishingly flexible in the midst of their own activities, so astonishing in every way. My God, I thought, I'm lucky to have these friends. It wasn't luck at all. It was grace, pure grace.

Erik and I often sat at a table in the garden and talked...and talked.... He talked, never verbosely, about things he knew almost everything about. I talked, always verbosely, about things I knew almost nothing about. The most memorable conversation was about "monotheism and schizophrenia." We weren't equals – but he gave me such a sense of equality with him. It wasn't a pose or a device. It was the authentic and unvarying Erik Erikson. He was always the listener, always the learner, always happy to be lowly. (Incidentally, I watched him with other people and concluded that he made everybody, kids and grown-ups alike, feel that nobody else could possibly be more interesting.) Because of his attentiveness and responsiveness and understanding and humor and reverence for what's holy about you, you could feel yourself coming to life. You religious people, bound as you are to forgive others, will forgive me for admitting that I always felt as if I were in the presence of God. I wasn't really confused between the two – and yet I *was* confused between the two, the One being somehow and wonderfully incarnate in the other. I hasten to mention that Erik wasn't confused. God was God, and he was he.

One afternoon, as we sat at that table in the garden, drinking dark beer and smoking cigarillos (the elements of our very private and very holy communion), we were just speculating about things. Since there seemed to be no limit to our speculations, I, jokingly, said, "Erik, when you get to heaven and meet God, what's the first thing you're going to say?" Immediately, and with charming wistfulness, he said, "Pardon me, Sir." There are (at least) two nuances to that. I suspect that he had both in mind.

Some things truly beautify human character. Integrity does. He had it. For instance, he refused to sign that "loyalty oath" when he was teaching at UC-Berkeley. He saw – and foresaw – how some of our compromises and compliances can tend toward evil, toward the destruction of persons and a whole society. And humility beautifies our character. Did he have that! Success – fame – didn't spoil him. It couldn't spoil him. And he spent his whole life contemplating the immensity in the heart of a child. Maybe that's why it was so easy for him to do a childlike thing at St. Stephen's Church in Belvedere, California, every Christmas Eve: play one of the three "Wise Men" in the Christmas pageant. (We were accused of typecasting him, and we never bothered to deny it.) If he didn't believe it in the depth of his own heart – which I'm absolutely sure he did – Joan kept reminding him that "unless you become as a little child, you shall never enter the kingdom of Heaven."

Because I loved being with Erik and Joan so much – because I loved them so much – I often volunteered to take them to the San Francisco International Airport when they were going on trips. They never asked. They didn't have to. I was at my own service by being at theirs. Once, as we were going up the Waldo Grade on Highway 101 in Marin County, I noticed that a highway patrolman had stopped a pretty blonde who was driving a red Volkswagen. Innocently – or should I say "unconsciously"? – I said, "Erik, have you ever noticed that highway patrolmen stop pretty blondes who drive red Volkswagens?" There was a moment of intense thoughtfulness, then a penetrating glint, then the verdict: "(A) that may be true," he said, "(B) you notice more." But comments like that never had any judgment in them. With me anyway, he was often amusedly serious – or seriously amused. It finally dawned on me that this great man was funny. Did he agree with Belloc, that "It's hardly worth the wear of winning, Save for laughter and the love of friends?" In any case, his rule seemed to be: be charitable. Be charitable to others. Be charitable with yourself. That charity, that divine *caritas* incarnate in him (and in Joan) made it possible for me to be *and* to become. The greatest spurts in my growth were the direct result of the sacred play of friendship with the Eriksons.

In 1975, six of us (the Eriksons, the Schoenbruns and we) went to Spain, on a kind of pilgrimage into the minds and hearts of St. Teresa of Avila and St. John of the Cross. In Spain, I became aware of Erik's limitless curiosity and of his reverential, perpetually awestruck, stance in the midst of this continuing and continuous creation. He gave you the impression that he was just bowled over by what people can do in this world. There wasn't any separating theirs from divine impulses. We walked through the Prado, side by side. There were long silences – he was never terrorized by silence – and occasional comments, about a Goya painting, about a Rivera painting, about a Bruegel painting. Each comment was revelation for me. To use the words of the title of one of his own books, he had "a way of looking at things." At El Escorial, we came upon some of the journals of St. Teresa in a glass case. He bent over it and gazed at the handwritten pages for a long, long time. He seemed to be reading every word, noticing how she dotted her i's and crossed her t's. Then he stood straight up, faced me, and said, "She must have been just about the most balanced human being who ever lived." There he was, centuries later, affirming a saint.

It was never possible for me to think of Erik apart from Joan. Maybe it was never possible for Erik to think of himself apart from Joan. Whenever he spoke about her, it wasn't just respectfully and appreciatively. Nor was it just reverently. It was with utter astonishment, that there could be such a person in this world – and in his life! Though they had been married for decades, he could be just as smitten as he was the night they met. And, occasionally, incredulous. I went to their house on Centro West in Tiburon early one summer morning, at the time when they were having their kitchen remodeled. Joan and a carpenter were in the kitchen, and Joan was telling the carpenter exactly what he had done wrong and exactly how he was going to fix it right away. I thought it best not to interrupt; so I stood as far away as possible, by the stairs going up to the bedroom. Suddenly, Erik appeared on the stairs, in bathrobe and slippers. He didn't say a word to me. He just listened for a while; then, beaming, he said, "I'm married to that woman!" Yes, he was married to that woman. And, for all his wisdom, he couldn't possibly have been wise enough to have chosen her decades before. (Nor she him.) One just has to conclude that they were chosen for each other, as we Church-people say, "before the foundation of the world." It was surely the work of Providence. Such a collaboration and communion of beings I had never witnessed before. They made sense out of the biblical statement that "the two of them shall become one." They were joint and fervent seekers after the same Good, the same Beauty, the same Truth. The *shekinah* of God shimmered and shone around them.

Religious people – some of whom are experts at what Erik called "superspeciation" (and, therefore, not very good at unconditional and carefree loving) – would like to claim and to capture this man. He belonged to us! Please… Though informed by many religions, he conformed only to the Spirit that, yes, infuses them, but transcends them all. He belonged to God. And he belonged to humanity: to you, every one of you…to Martin Luther and Mahatma Gandhi and the Yurok nation in northern California…to old people and to youth and to children, to everyone at every stage in life…to all the wounded ones of the world…to the spiritual giants, like St. Teresa of Avila and Martin Buber…to Jews and Christians and Hindus and to everyone who hankers for the holy…to Vienna and Cambridge and Berkeley and Tiburon and Harwich, this little town where he came to die. He belonged to something huge. Maybe a Rilke poem, which Joan translated, says it best:

"Everything will be huge and powerful again.
The lands simple and the waters rippled,
the trees enormous and the walls very low;
and in the valleys, strong and diverse,
a race of shepherds and tillers of the soil.

And no churches, which fence God in
like a fugitive and then harass him
like a trapped and wounded animal –
the houses hospitable to all knocking
and a sense of boundless self-offering
in every action and in you and in me….

His and Joan's house was certainly hospitable to my knocking. And there I learned that there's no fencing God in. And there I learned that only a boundless self-offering will ever bind us together. And there I learned that, some day, "everything will be huge and powerful again." At least, he, Erik Erikson, will remain "huge and powerful" in my life…and in yours…and in the lives of hundreds, of thousands of others across America and around the world. We all grieve; but, even at the grave, we sing our song, Alleluia, alleluia, alleluia! – and "on then with the dance."

The Rt. Rev. John S. Thornton, Bishop
Episcopal Diocese of Idaho
Boise, Idaho
Eulogy at Erik Erikson's Memorial Service
Harwich, Massachusetts
May 1994

Good Seed And Zizania

Today's gospel is in two parts. The first part is the parable that's attributed to Jesus, and I think it should be. It seems to me that it's characteristic of him. The Jesus Seminar scholars don't think it's authentic, but I disagree. The second part is the early Church's application of that parable, to answer the question, How do we live with the evil that's in the world?

Today's gospel is a simple story. A landowner (farmer) has his hired men scatter "good seed" in his field. Good seed? Ha! In those days, there was no such thing as good, clean, weed-free seed. There isn't these days either, in spite of all our technology. Take it from me. But to the naked eye, it sure looked good, and everybody was happy and full of hope. And, by golly, it came up and turned the field green with, it seemed, emeralds. Success. However, according to the text, there was somebody out there who had it in for the landowner. While the landowner was getting his zzz's and dreaming away, the person described as "an enemy" slipped into his field in the dark of the night and flung weed seed all over the place. Now it wasn't just any kind of weed seed; it was a particular kind of weed seed called "zizania" (the Greek word). Throughout the early stages of growth, one couldn't tell the grain from the zizania. It was a completely fraudulent plant. An OSU agronomy professor, down on his hands and knees with a magnifying glass, couldn't have told the difference. It was only when the plants began to mature that the difference could be told.

Gosh darn it, the hired men yelled, only they said it in Aramaic, which I won't quote. It shouldn't be repeated in polite company; and, besides, I don't know any Aramaic. However, I do know the language of farmers and farmhands when things go wrong. So the hired men hustled off to the landowner's house and banged on the door, still muttering Gosh darn it in Aramaic, and, breathlessly, said, We thought you gave us good seed to scatter in the field. Where did this blankety-blank zizania come from? Most commentators say that it really was an act of sabotage. According to them, it happened frequently back in those days, and there was even a law against it. So the landowner's suspicion that "an enemy did this" makes sense. But I have a very different idea about this parable. I think Jesus was being funny. How can you be the Messiah and not have a sense of humor, be, as we've said since ancient times, "fully human?" The landowner's response is in a category with Flip Wilson's "the Devil made me do it." Everybody laughs because everybody knows that the "Devil" didn't make him do it. He did it and knows he did it. In this case, the excited hired men say, Do you want us to find the dirty bugger who did this and beat the daylights out of him and make him pull up all the zizania and...? The landowner just smiles the smile of experience and laughs the laugh of wisdom. He knows that all you have to do is mention the word "enemy" and everybody gets paranoid and vengeful and nutty. No, he says, this happens every year. It's nature; and nature is more for us than against us. It's just something we have to live with. So let's hang on, and we'll do whatever we have to do at harvest time. Okay?

Among the real scholars, the German New Testament scholar Gunther Bornkamm, makes good sense. He says that this parable is about "reticence" and restraint. We just have to wait until it's perfectly clear to us that evil is evil before we speak out and start up-rooting it. That doesn't mean that there isn't evil in the world. There sure is. Not everybody is nice. There are some really nasty people around. There are people who love to hate, and some of them love to destroy property and kill others. For them, there just has to be a continual apocalypse run by the police and the courts. Even though the newspapers and TV keep us aware of all that, our lives are, I hope, much simpler. Still, we have to learn how to discern the real difference between good and evil. Getting all self-righteous and zealous and crazy can lead to more evil. To many religious people, it's always the Judgment Day. We have to do something about this right now! Jesus' response might be, Cool it. Wait a while. Let's be sure about this before we act foolishly.

We just have to get good at discernment. And how do we do that? Jesus is the Risen Human Being. He's the discernment, by his life and by his teaching, particularly the Sermon on the Mount and the Sermon on the Plain, most particularly the Beatitudes. We aren't very likely to get good at discernment until we meditate on him and his teaching on a daily basis. Gradually, we will rise with Him.

In thinking about this parable, a couple of things come to mind.

Parenthetically, it relates to foreign and military policy. If you set out to capture or kill terrorists (zizania), you're bound to kill a lot of innocent people (good grain) at the same time. It calls for restraint.

Everybody knows that the Anglican Communion is in crisis these days. We can make it our own crisis if we want to. I won't. God, as I understand God, can use the Anglican Communion wondrously and has and probably will for a long time; but God, as I understand God, isn't dependent on the Anglican Communion or any other human institution. It's not a time to get all self-righteous and zealous and crazy. Largely because we have a female Presiding Bishop and a gay bishop in New Hampshire – though there are other issues, revolving around authority and power – some of the primates in what's called the "Global South" have accused us and the Canadian Anglicans of promoting a "false gospel" and living it defiantly. We're the zizania; they're the good grain. This parable is in the Bibles they read and in the Bibles we read. I say it's about reticence and restraint until the "harvest," whenever that is, God only knows. They say the "harvest" has come and we have to be uprooted. They read the Bible selectively, but I read the Bible selectively too. But I don't live where they live, and they don't live where I live; so I can't judge them, and their judging me is possibly more than God would do. I assume that they're trying their best to be faithful to Christ and to each other, though they'll never do it perfectly; and I wish they'd make the same assumption about me and you and everybody else in the Communion. I don't want to belong to a Church that produces wing nuts. (In addition to being the nuts on bolts, "wing nuts," a new term in the new Merriam-Webster Dictionary, are people who always propose the most radical solutions to problems.)

The biggest issue, which this parable brings up, is about me. It could be about you too, and I suspect it is. The question for me is, Is there anything I'm saying or doing that isn't consistent with the life and teaching of Jesus, the Risen Human Being? If I find anything in me that perpetuates or is complicit in evil, I have to pull it up, burn it up, get it out of the field of my life. There's zizania in me. For me, every day is harvest time. I'm not fully transformed into the likeness of Christ, but I intend to be. I suspect I've only just begun; but as St. Paul said of himself, I know what the goal is, and so I press on.

The Rt. Rev. John S. Thornton
St. Mary's Episcopal Church
Eugene, Oregon
July 20, 2008

Tell Them They'll See Him In Hailey, Idaho

Alleluia, Christ is risen!
The Lord is risen indeed, alleluia!

If you come to church every Sunday (or almost every Sunday), thanks for being here again. If you come to church only at Christmas and Easter, thanks for coming. You grace our lives. If this is the first time you've ever been in church, we consider you sent by God to bless us. This is the question: Can we all, in this moment, be one in the breaking of bread? There is only one universal way of saying, "I love you," and that's in the breaking of bread, all of us sharing one loaf, all of us drinking from one cup. Let's do it!

(By the way, if any – or all – of this is new to you, just do what everybody else does. You'll be just fine. It isn't magic.)

There's going to be a lot of verbiage in the next ten or twelve minutes – you'll be lucky if it's only that long – but I want you to go away with twenty-nine words in your memory. I know it sounds grammar school-ish, but repeat just four phrases after me:

If you have eyes to see him,

you will see him everywhere.

If you have the heart to be like him,

you can be like him anywhere.

Let's do that one more time.

(It's repeated, boisterously.)

The Resurrection is about our humanity. Today is the Day of Resurrection. Yesterday was the Day of Resurrection. Tomorrow will be the Day of Resurrection. Any and every day can be the Day of Resurrection because the Resurrection is about how we live our lives in this world. That's the story of the gospels, Matthew, Mark, Luke and John.

You can't nail the Spirit of Christ to a cross. You can't wrap the Spirit of Christ in a shroud. You can't lay the Spirit of Christ in a tomb and roll a stone over the entrance. You can't station guards in front so that nobody can get access. Heavens, say Matthew, Mark, Luke and John, the Spirit of Christ will burst out of there and roam and race through the world, laughing or weeping according to the condition of persons, affirming life.

It's rank literalism that ruins the story for us. We keep saying, "He is risen from the dead," "He is risen from the dead," "He is risen from the dead." Well, he *is* risen from the dead. So who are the dead? The dead are all those who don't or won't love when it's perfectly clear that only love will ever get us out of the deadly cycle of retribution and violence. The dead are all those who don't have the nerve to be unworldly when the world will accept, even applaud, hate. The dead are those who take some aspect of some religion and use it to make their last stand against God. (You know I'm thinking of ISIS.)

Story after story after story in the gospels is about Jesus saying or doing something that compelled people to say, one way or another, "He's risen in the midst of those who are dead. That includes us. We've been dead too. But he's alive; so let's follow him into life."

What's true of Jesus is true of anyone who has a heart such as his. In the last chapter of Mark's Gospel, there's this phrase: "...And he appeared in the form of a stranger...." And there's a footnote in one of the gospel accounts of the Resurrection, referring to an ancient manuscript, "...And he appeared in many other forms also." Of course! The Spirit of Christ is forever taking the form of someone who loves God and neighbor above all loves. There's no reason why the Spirit of Christ can't take the form of YOU.

(I go out into the congregation, to ask several persons for their first names.)

"What's your first name?"

(The person gives me his first name.)

"There's no reason why the Spirit of Christ shouldn't appear to us in _____."

What's your first name?"

(The person gives me her first name.)

"There's no reason why the Spirit of Christ shouldn't appear to us in _____."

"What's your first name?"

(The person gives me his first name.)

"There's no reason why the Spirit of Christ shouldn't appear to us in _____."

Do you get it?

In Matthew's Gospel, an angel tells Mary Magdalene and "the other Mary" (whoever that was) – I'll paraphrase now – "Get going! Tell those disciples that he's not in this tomb. He's on his way to Galilee and they'll see him there." I'll paraphrase that one more time, with absolute fidelity to the meaning of the text: "Get going! Tell those disciples that he's not in this tomb. He's on his way to Hailey, Idaho, and they'll see him there." Hailey, Idaho, the place of Resurrection. Would you believe it? Would you? Keep your eyes open, my loves. You'll see him here.

It's all about how we live our lives in this world. It's all about our capacity for love, for forgiveness, for mercy, for empathy, for generosity, for sacrifices that cost us something, for kindly laughter that dispels the darkness, for simple caring for one another and for this imperiled planet. When you see these things in anyone, you see the Risen Christ. And when people see these things in you, they will know that you too are risen from the dead. Alleluia!

Back to what I want you to remember. Repeat after me, just one last time:

If you have eyes to see him,

you will see him everywhere.

If you have the heart to be like him,

you can be like him anywhere.

Now, let's break bread and have brunch, then get going and tell everyone that they'll see him right here in Hailey, Idaho.

The Rt. Rev. John S. Thornton
Emmanuel Episcopal Church
Hailey, Idaho
Easter Day 2016

Clothed With Christ

Well, we made it through Hallowe'en. The decorations are off the front porch and the lawn. The costumes are put away. There's still half a bowl of candy to eat up or give away. It was all lots of fun and a good way to let some of the mischief and weirdness out of our systems.

"Halloween" is nearly always misspelled. It should be "Hallowe'en" with an apostrophe between the first "e" and the second "e." The apostrophe takes the place of the "v" in "even." It's the even-ing before All Hallows Day. You just about have to be a churchgoing member of a liturgical church to know that. However, the misspelling is now standard usage, and the world doesn't care if it makes me crabby.

Hallowe'en has a long history and innumerable traditions. At one time in its history, the revellers ventured into cemeteries at night and put dishes of milk by the graves, so that the dead, when they rose, would have something to drink. It's the rankest superstition, of course, but there is a truth tucked away in it. Genetically and psychologically, the dead do "rise" in us and live in us. There is a sense in which my dad and mom, long since dead, still live in me. They still tell me what to do and what not to do, God bless them. In fact, that's the whole point of Christianity, that the crucified Christ will rise in us and live in us and, through us, proclaim that love is the Way.

(By the way, I have a friend in Forest Grove who, every year, goes to her mother's grave somewhere down there in Texas and pours a bottle of her mother's favorite single-malt scotch on the grave, with affection and gratitude and the mother's mischief still alive in the daughter.)

So All Hallows Day it is, and you're the hallowed ones. We call it All Saints Day now, and you're the sainted ones. Sainted, sanctified you are. Your names aren't in *Holy Women and Holy Men* or *Lesser Feasts and Fasts* or *The Book of Common Prayer*, but this day is as much about you as it is about the people who get their names in books. At Baptism, with Chrism, the cross of Christ was burned into your foreheads; and, though no one can see it, you know it's there. And I remind you that, at Baptism, you received the "Seven Gifts of the Holy Ghost." In case you've forgotten – or never knew – what they are, I'll tell you: Wisdom, Understanding, Counsel, Fortitude, Knowledge, Piety and Fear of the Lord. How are you doing with the gifts you were given? I'm a little short on all of them, particularly "Piety." However, I'm trying to do better.

The Gospel lesson for All Saints Day is the story of the raising of Lazarus, from John's Gospel. In the 1928 *Book of Common Prayer*, the Gospel lesson was always the Beatitudes, in Matthew 5. I'd prefer the Beatitudes over the Lazarus story. The Beatitudes need to be drilled into us:

"Blessed are the poor in spirit."
"Blessed are the meek."
"Blessed are the merciful."
Etc.
"Blessed are the peacemakers."

I was, I admit, mystified by the Standing Liturgical Commission's choice of John 11:33-44, the raising of Lazarus, as the Gospel lesson for All Saints Day. Why? Why not?

We American Christians are so afflicted by biblical literalism. We have to believe that Lazarus was dead, wrapped up in a shroud, laid in a tomb, closed in the darkness forever, to become nothing but a pile of bones. But let's reimagine this. I'm not asking you to concur with me. You can do your own hermeneutic. You're smart people.

Suppose Lazarus wasn't dead. Suppose he was just a deadbeat. He had always been a deadbeat, say, living off his sisters, Mary and Martha. He was a moocher, a leech, a sponge, a lazy good-for-nothing bum. He had mastered the manipulation of his sisters, who went on enabling his deadbeat existence, with pity that outweighed their disgust. Ask Mary what she thought about Lazarus and she'd say, "He stinks." Ask Martha what she thought about Lazarus and she'd say, "He stinks." Their brother was a rotten human being. Still, Mary's and Martha's behavior didn't change; so his didn't either. Are you still with me on this flight of imagination?

When Jesus came to town, those dear sisters said, "If you had just come sooner, you might have made Lazarus as alive as you are. As it is, he's just going to rot away."

"Where is he now?"

"God only knows. For all the good he does, he might as well be in a tomb. He must be somewhere around. Just call him."

"Lazarus, come out!!! There's living to do. I'll show you how."

(I want you to experience the power of that command. When I count to three, we'll all shout, "Lazarus, come out!" One...two... three. "Lazarus, come out!")

From wherever he was, out he came, like a man rising from the dead; and, in the presence of the one who is fully alive, saying, "Show me."

"Take up your cross (yourself), Lazarus, and follow me. Whoever loses his life for my sake and the Gospel's finds it."

There's a little bit of Lazarus in every one of us that needs to be called out.

Notice the very last sentence in the Gospel lesson: "Unbind him, and let him go." It's an order; it's a command; it's not an option. "Unbind him!" Jesus was always doing that. To Jairus' daughter, who they thought was "dead," he said, "Get up!" To the paralytic whose buddies hauled him off to the place where Jesus was teaching, he said, "Get up!" To the lame man who, day after day, lay by the pool of Siloam, waiting for an angel to stir the healing waters, he said, "Get up!" That's not exactly an example of nondirective counseling. Anyway, the command to "unbind" him was a command to Mary and Martha and all the townspeople. You see, with our perceptions and judgments and avoidance – and our gossip – we do bind each other. You are only what I think you are and you'll never be anything more. I'll never see the image of God in you. Now that's the attitude that "binds" people, wraps them in shrouds, lays them in tombs, closes them in the darkness, God help us. One way or another, our message must be, Come out! Be alive! Claim your individuality!

After having said all that, I'm not going to preach about the raising of Lazarus. It's All Saints Day. This is the day when we commemorate everyone who was ever baptized. It would be good if, on this one day during the Liturgical Year, we were to wear white, as on the day of Baptism.

Back in the days of the 1928 *Book of Common Prayer*, we wore white on Whitsunday (or White Sunday). Remembering that those early converts to the Way, after having been baptized (by immersion), were dressed in white, the color of the new life in Christ; and, in the community of the Beloved, resisting ever to be discolored by the world. Whitsunday is the same as Pentecost; but, over the decades of the Twentieth Century, "Whitsunday" dropped out of our liturgical lexicon and, now, it's just "Pentecost." Instead of wearing white, we wear red, making ourselves flames of fire and, together, a refining fire. I wish. I wish all of Eugene would say, "Wow! Those people at St. Thomas are on fire!"

It wasn't just ritual and symbolism for those Jesus People in the First Century. After long and intense preparation, they were ready to live in the world but not of it. They had been, to use St. Paul's language, "clothed with Christ." What a concept. I'm not talking about wardrobe; I'm talking about a new way of living in the world.

Paul, in his letter to the Galatians, says "For as many of you who were baptized into Christ have put on Christ." That's you. You've put on Christ. You're wearing Christ. And because you're wearing Christ, you're part of the community of radical equality. Paul goes on: "There is neither Jew nor Greek, there is neither slave nor free, there is neither male nor female; for you are all one in Christ Jesus" (Galatians 3:28). Those who wear Christ are called the "Church."

In another context (Colossians 3:10, 12-17), Paul says, Take off your old nature and put on the new nature (i.e., be clothed with Christ). Take off the rags of the world, particularly our compliance with violence in any of its forms. Paul gets very specific about what your new nature is. You've put on "compassion," "kindness," "lowliness," "meekness," "patience," and thankfulness – and forgiveness, to the extent that you yourselves have been forgiven. Try to remember how many times. "And above all," says Paul, "put on love, which binds everything together in perfect harmony... And let the peace of Christ rule in your hearts, to which indeed you were called in the one body."

Given all that, how am I doing? How are you doing? How are we all doing as a church? Do people who come here for the first time say, I don't know what they were wearing, but it was beautiful. I want to wear what they wear.

Remembering who we are by Baptism, let's clothe ourselves with Christ.

The Rt. Rev. John S. Thornton
St. Thomas Episcopal Church
Eugene, Oregon
November 1, 2015

It's Your Call

From the command center comes a voice, modulated to nearly a whisper, "It's your call." So...it was his call, to pull the trigger or not...to end a life or not. A couple of hundred times, it was his call. A couple of hundred times, he pulled the trigger. A couple of hundred times, a life was ended.

—◊—

When, on the Internet, I saw the trailer for Clint Eastwood's *American Sniper*, I was dazed by that line ("It's your call.") Oh, I thought, this is a movie about moral decision-making, split-second decision-making, day-after-day split-second decision-making. I need to see that. (I'm always looking for homiletical material.) I told Jan I wanted to see the movie. She, who goes everywhere with me, told me, flatly, that I could go alone. (She did not say, If you go, don't come back, however. Unconditional love is what it is. I'm used to it – but I never take it for granted. Nor do I test it.) So I became ambivalent about going to the movie, especially all alone – or at all. Finally, I decided not to go, though not because Jan wouldn't go with me. I had another reason.

In the trailer, the sniper is perched on a rooftop in some Iraqi city. A boy clutching what looks like a mortar shell is in his sights. The boy's mother, she who gave him birth, she who could foresee his manhood, proudly, is standing beside him. From the command center comes a voice, modulated nearly to a whisper, "It's your call."

So…it was his call, to pull the trigger – or not…to end a life – or not. He pulled the trigger. He ended a life, a boy's (though the trailer doesn't show that). As fast as a bullet, I, with horror, realized that, in some unconverted and nearly implacable place in my being, I may still, oh, still, believe that violence can be redemptive. Could it be hard-wired in the human psyche, there since Cain killed Abel? However, as was said after that "war to end all wars," believing that violence can be redemptive is "The Grand Illusion." Violence begets violence, over and over again, endlessly, save for the high courage of forgiveness. I believe that, but it's something I continually have to re-learn and for which I have to seek affirmation from sympathetic Christians – and sympathetic Jews and Muslims. I yearn for the day when we'll all say, There is no justification for violence. Isaiah did. Jeremiah did. Amos did. Micah did. Jesus, whom we call "Lord," did. So what about us?

Last weekend, Americans spent 15.2 million dollars on tickets to *American Sniper.* It has been nominated for five different Academy Awards. According to David Denby, who does movie reviews for *The New Yorker,* Clint Eastwood's "command of the material makes most directors look like beginners." As Jake Coyle, who writes for the Associated Press, says, "Clint Eastwood has again lapped his younger colleagues, this time with his best movie in years." By contemporary American standards, it's a good movie, maybe a great one. Who besides my wife can resist it?

American Sniper is an accolade for an American sniper's singular, unexceptionable skill with a high-powered rifle and, at the same time, a kind of dirge for the same sniper's solitary, unutterable misery. It's based on the 2012 best-selling autobiography of Navy SEAL

Chris Kyle. (I haven't read it.) In U.S. military history, there's never been a sniper quite like him. Evidently, unperturbed, he made 160 confirmed kills and more than 200 probable kills. I read that his father had taught him about "the gift of aggression" and the obligation to defend others, "others" having a narrow definition, only the "good guys." To a moral certainty, he was sure that he was defending U.S. troops – and America – against the "bad guys," and, at least in one instance, a "bad kid." "Savages," he called them. But each time he killed, he died too.

Eastwood is a storyteller and a movie-maker and provocateur. *American Sniper* is both a war movie and an anti-war movie at the same time. Just as he did in *Pale Rider* (my favorite) and *The Unforgiven*, he intends, it seems to me, for theater-goers to leave theaters with a troubled mind and a troubled conscience and baffled and bamboozled by human existence. The good person is capable of violence, and the violent person is capable of repentance. Maybe his question is, Will we ever be reborn?

People can find plenty of reasons for going to *American Sniper*. I have one for not going. I could find the time. I have the money. And I have a high degree of curiosity, maybe even voyeurism. But, lying in bed before the morning light one day, I decided, firmly, not to lend my soul to the darkness of the world. I'm not asking you to agree with me. As an old man, I don't seek agreement anymore. I speak from my heart. I'm just saying that what I make of my life is my call. Not going to *American Sniper* is my call. (I already know that the objections and arguments will come flying. I'm not trying to run a Legion of Decency here. I'm just telling you where I feel called to make a stand.)

The movie is about a man, probably a Christian man, though I don't know that, who methodically kills 160 to 200 Iraqis, surely every one of them a Muslim. If I were an American Muslim, how would I feel about that? Can I learn to feel what they feel? This is my country, but those are my people, they might say. It makes me sad, they might say. It makes me angry, they might say. That sadness and that anger would surely multiply and deepen and, over the months and years, get beyond the reach of consciousness and positive expression and constructive action.

I don't think *American Sniper* is in a category with Charlie Hebdo's m.o., of derision and insults and ridicule and contempt and humiliation and mockery and, in the minds of many, blasphemy and, as *The New Yorker* writer Adam Gopnik says, "the job of ignobility." The Prophet Muhammad wasn't the only object of it all; so was the Pope. It was not gentle, benign satire. With "the freedom of speech," they were testing, testing the limits of tolerance. The reaction was understandable, but not justified. It lit a conflagration around the world. In Niger last week, ten Christians were killed, dozens injured, and forty-five churches set on fire. Exactly how were they responsible for Charlie Hebdo? Without the Golden Rule fixed in every heart, the world goes insane. It reminded me of a line from last Sunday's reading from First Corinthians: "All things are lawful for me, but not all things are beneficial." Just because we have rights doesn't mean that we have to exercise them, the results be damned.

We just have to find a way to live with each other in spite of our many differences, of race, of ethnicity, of nationality, of gender-identity, of religion, of everything. Those of us who aren't radicalized have to lead the way. Those of us who live in this pluralistic democracy have to show the world that it can be done. And what's the use of the Church if it isn't in the vanguard of peacemaking, always crossing the boundaries set by fear and hatred and revenge to behold the essential sacredness of the other? What's the use?

The relations of Christians and Muslims – and Jews – don't have to be stuck in the Twelfth and Thirteenth Centuries. The memory of the Crusades seems never to fade. However, there was once a beautiful moment centuries before.

According to Kamran Pasha, the author of *The Mother of Believers*, "Seventh Century Arabia would make modern Afghanistan look like an advanced civilization." A man named Muhammad had a vision of the Angel Gabriel telling him that God had sent him to lead the Arabs out of darkness into light. The time had come for the Arabs to rejoin the children of Abraham in worshipping the One God, the God of Moses and Jesus. The movement became known as "Islam," which means "to surrender oneself to God." The first followers were the poor, many of them slaves, with a few greathearted merchants. But the new faith was ridiculed and, soon, persecuted by Muhammad's own tribe.

By C.E. 615, the persecution became a matter of life or death. Facing the probability of extinction, about eighty Muslims, led by Muhammad's daughter and son-in-law, fled to Abyssinia (Ethiopia today). Because trade with Africa was so essential to Arabia, having dissenting Arabs in Abyssinia could be a great hindrance to merchants. A delegation, laden with the material of bribes, was sent to the king of Abyssinia, Negus, to persuade him to expel the "trouble-makers." When called to court, the Muslims explained that they had no intention of making trouble for anyone. They were there to escape persecution. The Prophet's cousin stepped up and made the following speech:

"O King, we were people steeped in ignorance, worshipping idols...Thus we were until God sent us a Messenger from out of our midst, one whose lineage we knew...He called us unto God that we should testify to His Oneness and worship Him and renounce what we and our fathers had worshipped in the way of stones and idols; and he commanded us to speak truly to fulfill our promises, to respect the ties of kinship and the rights of our neighbors, and to refrain from crimes and bloodshed. So we worship God alone, setting naught beside Him, counting as forbidden what He has forbidden and as licit what He has allowed. For these reasons have our people turned against us, and have persecuted us to make us forsake our religion and revert from the worship of God to the worship of idols. That is why we have come to your country...."

King Negus was intrigued. He asked their spokesman to recite something from the Qur'an. So he recited the stories of the Annunciation of the Virgin Mary and the Nativity of Jesus, right out of the Qur'an. That did it. "Go your way," he said, "you are safe in my country. Not for a mountain of gold would I harm a single one of you."

It could be said, I think without overstatement or hyperbole, that King Negus and the Christians of Abyssinia helped to save early Islam. (I do have to admit, however, that some of the bishops put up a short fight over some of the fine points of doctrine. The king simply overruled them.) If not of one mind, the Christians and the Muslims were of one heart.

Muslims live among us here in Boise and we among them. This is Boise. This isn't Paris, France. This is Boise, Idaho. This is the place and this is the time for a radical commitment to neighborliness. We don't have to get caught up in the world's madness. We can learn to approach each other respectfully and appreciatively and joyfully. We can live in peace if we intend to, though not without continual effort. This community will be what we make of it. It's as if a voice comes from heaven, modulated to nearly a whisper, "It's your call." It's your call. It's mine. It's ours, always to give life to each other — or not.

The Rt. Rev. John S. Thornton
St. Michael's Cathedral
Boise, Idaho
January 25, 2014

Between Harvest And Winter

Maybe the reason why so few people are going to see the movie *Country* these days is that so few people live in it. Live in the country, I mean. Out there where corn grows, row against row, from farmhouse to horizon. And out there where a boy, still three years away from getting even a learner's permit, commandeers a Farmall down and back, down and back, from chores to dusk, under a blistering sun, cultivating. And out there where God works silently and secretly in the darkness of sticky summer nights. It's what I used to call "America," and the very word was a kind of song that sang itself in me, in the me that nobody had ever transported beyond glorious cornfields before. Sure, I knew that there were cities, big cities, some of which were bulging bigger than a country boy's imagination gone wild. Like Chicago. And New York. And Los Angeles, which was somewhere out there on the West Coast, near Hollywood. But it took me years to believe that people actually lived in them. And ate corn, too. The city and the country were two totally different realities, and alien. And one can go right on thinking that, until, over boyhood's horizon at last, say at thirty-three thousand feet some day, he can look down and see it all. And can see that it's all one. The whole country is country, really.

From city limits to city limits, America is a farm.

So we went from the country where we live, silver in snow and moonlight that night, to *Country* on the silver screen, my wife and teenage daughter and I. Having read maybe half a dozen reviews in newspapers and magazines – none of which, I swear, was written by any legitimate person, like someone with even the faint memory of a little cow manure caked to his boots – we decided to go anyway. That is, my wife and I decided to. Our daughter had no choice, and so protested all the way. "Why should I have to go to a dumb movie about farmers?" she grumped. (At fifteen, the center of her universe is in town, at the Catholic high school, with her friends.) The justifications rolled off my tongue, from "We hicks have to look out for each other." to "We just can't stand to be without you." Nothing worked. But, once inside the lobby of the theater, with a eucharist of popcorn and Pepsi, she was perfectly compliant and just as eager as we to find out what Hollywood could do with this crisis in some farmers' lives. And in America's life. Many, obviously, didn't share that eagerness. The theater was nine-tenths empty. There we sat, the three of us, almost alone, in a stubble of unoccupied, forsaken seats, as if in a cornfield between harvest and winter. The house lights faded into a licorice night, before day burst and a frozen beauty on the screen. Within seconds, that sense of loneliness was overwhelmed by this heroic film about some heroic people. Our daughter was the first to exclaim so – and to demand to go a second time, with her friends from the Catholic high school in town.

That's when I knew that *Country* was an even better movie than I thought. It wasn't all my concern and all my politics and all my nostalgia – and my knowing best what kind of movies teenage girls ought to see. Why, that girl wouldn't have been more transfixed if Michael Jackson himself had moonwalked through the muck of the Ivys' cow yard, in a brand new pair of LaCrosse knee-highs. No matter what other moviegoers might think about *Country* – which could flop at the box offices, like a sow into

a mudhole – she's not going to forget it. Or the Carter grain em-
bargo. Or seventeen and a half percent interest rates. Or Jessica
Lange taking on FmHA. Nor will my wife. Nor will I. This movie has a message, and the message is urgent. It's this: either we're
going to have to have a darned good fight, in Congress, in state leg-
islatures, in courts, everywhere public policy is made, or we'll end
up at a funeral. The funeral will be for small (and middle-sized)
farms *and* small towns and small businesses and small schools and,
yes, small churches, too.

The Lord giveth. The fittest taketh away.

Jesse Helms may be wrong about many things, but he's sure
right about one: 1985 may be "the most crucial year for American
agriculture in this century." Everything I read, whether in *The
Kiplinger Agricultural Letter* or in a transcript of a *MacNeil-Lehrer Report*,
says as much. And these intuitions and anticipations and projections
are turning into prophecies, and the prophecies could easily be fulfilled, while we're all at the movies. Outside, where business is really done, the biggest transfer of wealth in the nation's history could
take place, from the many to the few. The few, with banks-full of
capital behind them, will floor their gleaming eighteen-wheelers
right through those old boundaries called The Democratic Process
and Community and Our Place and things oh so beautiful in their
smallness. As for the many, they'll have to go to the only place
there is to go, to hard and unyielding cities, to join the ranks of the
landless. We're at that point in history, says an article in the most
recent *Small Farm Advocate*, when America could "give up on the idea
that the people who work the land should also enjoy the rights and
responsibilities of owning it."

It's enough to make Thomas Jefferson rise up from the grave.

The Rt. Rev. John S. Thornton
Taucross Farm
Scio, Oregon
1985

Wimberley, Texas

I know what you're thinking. You're thinking, Where did Sandy dig up this old guy? Well, I'll tell you. Like a zillion famous potatoes, I was dug up from Idaho. Idaho. That's the state where even many Christians would like to add the Second Amendment to the Apostles Creed. Just in case God isn't our Protector, we need to be armed, they think. We can solve all our problems with lethal weapons. It's crazy. However, like everywhere, there are wonderful people in Idaho. It's a good place to live. It's just that no state in the Union bears any unmistakable resemblance to the kingdom of heaven, including Texas.

So this is the place Sandy crows about. She's happy to be here, and you should be happy to have her here. I'll tell you why. Persona and person don't always come together in the clergy of the Church. They do in her. What you see in public is what you'd see in private and vice versa. Persona and person, one and the same. And there is, definitely, a distinction between priest-craft and priesthood. Priest-craft is doing the job, even well; priesthood is having your whole heart in it. Sandy has her whole heart in it. What she does she does because she believes that Jesus is the Risen Human Being, risen right out of fallen humanity, to show us the new way of being human with the nature of the Divine. Read the Sermon on the Mount, especially the Beatitudes, every day, twice a day, until they become the song of your soul.

So this is the 25th Anniversary of the creation of the St. Stephen's Episcopal School. Are any present or former trustees here? Are any present or former faculty or staff here? Are any present or former students here? You're celebrating the fact – we're all celebrating the fact – that you never had any money troubles, never had any personnel problems, never had an issue that kept you up at night wondering why you ever got yourself into this. It has been a snap, hasn't it? Ha, you say, this man's a dreamer. He's a dunce. I am not!

Seventeen years ago, my wife, Jan, and I founded a day school for Indian kids who live on a reservation in eastern Idaho. They're some of the poorest but most beautiful kids in America – Shoshonis, Bannocks, with an Arapahoe or two and, maybe, a Pine Ridge Sioux thrown in. Their parents or whomever they live with at the moment don't have one thin dime for tuition; so there isn't any tuition. We have to raise about $300,000 a year. We're still at it, and a lot of people are still at it with us. We know that starting an Episcopal school and keeping it going payroll-by-payroll is about as complicated as a Moon-shot. Let me tell you, it *is* rocket science.

So, the students bless you, their parents bless you, the teachers and the staff bless you, this whole community of Episcopalian Christians, in God's name, blesses you.

Our daughter Julia and her husband, David, and their two children, Connor and Camille, live in El Segundo, California. It's a suburb of LA, out by the ocean, a lovely little town sandwiched between LAX and a Chevron refinery. They're happy there.

Julia isn't theologically educated, but she's theologically grounded. She was tutored at our table. Last summer, Julia's friends, also moms, told her about a very popular vacation Bible school at a local church. (I won't name the church – but I will tell you that it wasn't an Episcopal, Lutheran, Presbyterian, Methodist or Baptist church. It wasn't Roman Catholic either. I'll let you guess at what's left.) The moms said that their kids loved it because there were games and movies and refreshments and, of course, a few classes. So Julia gave in and took Connor and Camille there. They lasted one day. After that first day, they reported that their teacher told them – and I quote – "It's good to die and go to heaven because it's just like Hawaii." Heaven? Just like Hawaii? Though they'd never been to Hawaii, it didn't feel right to them – and it certainly didn't feel right to their mother. (If the children's teacher had said that heaven is just like Wimberley, Texas, she might not have made such a fuss.) Filling children's heads with thoughts of death and heaven was wrong. There was no second day in that vacation Bible school. A couple of days later, the director of the vacation Bible school phoned, to ask why her children didn't return. "I'm a Christian woman," Julia said, perhaps huffily, "and I know the difference between sound doctrine and nonsense." So she decided to take Connor and Camille ten miles away, in heavy LA traffic, to an Episcopal vacation Bible school. They liked it, and the refreshments were great.

It reminds me of the time Jan and I were walking in downtown Boise, near the Idaho Statehouse. We were untroubled and weren't looking for any when we encountered this evangelist. Evangelists come in all kinds of disguises. It never occurred to me that he might be one, built, as he was, like a cage fighter or, at least, someone a weak old man like me wouldn't want to tangle with. I made the mistake of smiling at the man and greeting him with "Good Morning" (which is my idea of evangelism). That did it. He was all over us. Now this may sound prideful and conceited and arrogant, but I don't think that Jan and I give the appearance of needing rescue from the brink of eternal perdition.

"I have good news for you," he said.

"What's the good news?" I asked, giving him permission to back us against the light post.

"Do you believe in Jesus Christ?" he asked.

I was tempted to say "No," just to escape what was beginning to feel like bullying; but I said "Yes" because I do believe in Jesus Christ. That's when I decided to take charge of the encounter, to put it pretty much on my terms, so that I could feel less, well, trapped.

"You're from Eastern Europe, aren't you?" I asked.

"The Ukraine," he said.

"How long have you lived in the U.S.?" I asked.

"Fifteen years," he said.

"Where do you live now?" I asked.

"Portland, Oregon." he said. "I go to a Bible college there."

"Good for you," I said, trying, honestly, to affirm him in doing what I don't do and never will.

"It's good to meet a believer," he said, seeing that we were slowing backing away, into the perils of the wicked city. Before we could get completely free, he handed me a tract. I took it, though I didn't want it, having been handed dozens of those things over the years. "Thanks," I said, "I'll read it."

At a safe distance, we stopped so that I could scan the tract. The cover read "DEATH – IT HAPPENS EVERY DAY," with a picture of the Grim Reaper, scythe in hand, on the front. I said to Jan, "I don't consider this good news."

Later in the day, I read the whole tract. "You can only get everlasting life by trusting Jesus," it said. "This is not just a co-incidence that you are reading this tract and not someone else," it went on. Then came the clincher: "This could be your last warning." My last warning? That I could die beyond the infinite love of God? Did I break out in a cold sweat? Heavens, no. Not a shiver, not a shake, not a fleeting thought about the frigidity of that warning.

I object to the manipulation of persons with the threat of death or the Last Judgment or Purgatory or Hell or the Rapture, when those of us who are left behind stand gazing at the rear ends of the righteous as they fly up to heaven. They proclaim an impatient, punitive, pathetic little god, the projection of meanness and nastiness and inferiority twisted into their brand of holiness. They try to scare the love of the world out of us, the very world, we're told, that God created and pronounced "good," the very one that Christ, for love, gave his life. "I have come that they may have life," he said, "and have it abundantly."

Abundant life. That's the gospel kids get at the St. Stephen's Episcopal School. Life is precious, invaluable. Be glad that you are you, the one and only you. Become everything you can become, incomparably, though humbly. Give your life for the life of the world. Don't be afraid to love God and your neighbor and yourself. Let the Risen Christ rise in you and bespeak a love that is healthy and happy and holy. (By the way, I found *the* existential question on the back wall of the Leaning Pear yesterday. Two lines from a Mary Oliver poem: "Tell me, what is it that you plan to do/with your one wild precious life?")

I've done a little research into public education in Wimberley, Texas. Good things are going on here. Your teachers stay a long time and they're pretty well paid – though not by comparison to Wyoming. Scores in reading, math, science and social studies are way up. Now listen to this: all eight sixth graders in the St. Stephen's Episcopal School were elected to the National Junior Honor Society! The high school completion rate in Wimberley is about as close to one hundred percent as any school district in America ever gets. Seventy percent of Wimberley High School graduates are college-ready in English language arts, seventy-three percent in math and sixty-two percent in both. How's that? Now compare it to Idaho, where college-readiness is only thirty-seven percent.

I'm a stranger here, but what that tells me is that you are achievers who expect achievement – and nurture achievement – and support achievement – and incite achievement – and praise achievement – and finance achievement. Of course, St. Stephen's Episcopal School stands for academic achievement. However, there's another kind of achievement for which the school exists, peculiarly and exceptionally.

What educators are telling us these days is that the development of cognitive skills is not more important than the formation of character. What's the point of being a whiz at math and science but totally disinterested in the lives of others, in the life of the community, in the life of the state and nation and world, in the life of the planet? It may be that the highest praise a kid can ever get is that he/she "plays well with others." I mean collaboratively; I mean joyfully; I mean generously; I mean ethically. They learn it more by watching than by listening. Kids learn that from grown-ups, mostly.

Years ago, I read an article by one of those deep-thinking guys, Reinhold Niebuhr or Paul Tillich or someone with a whole lot of authority, who said that, ultimately, relationships are more important than curricula. (That doesn't mean that curricula are unimportant.) I know it's true. I still remember my fifth grade teacher at the Lincoln Grade School in Elgin, Illinois, Mrs. Wondergem. How apt can a name be? And I remember Chet Alexander, the principal at the Elgin High School and my track coach. I remember Roy Battenhouse, my honors tutor at Indiana University. Every one of you remembers those who showed us how to live the good life that forms the good society.

The Head of School, the teachers, the aides, the whole staff of the St. Stephen's Episcopal School is a curriculum, showing succeeding generations that such love of which Jesus was the incarnation is "the way, the truth and life." By the time they leave this school they should love to love.

One last thing before I end.

A few months ago, I read a David Brooks column in *The New York Times*. He was writing about education, especially higher education, but it was all applicable to elementary and secondary education as well. He quoted a famous Harvard psychology professor. I won't soon forget what he said. He said, "We're good at teaching students. We're really good at it. But we don't know how to teach them to make a life worth living. We don't know how to teach them to make a soul." "Make a soul." That's a great old Anglican phrase and concept. From the day of our birth until this very second, each of us is in the process of making a soul, offering it to the world, offering it to God. You're here to do what the Harvard professor says he and his colleagues aren't able to do. In all that you do here at St. Stephen's Episcopal Church and at the St. Stephen's Episcopal School, you're teaching children how to make a soul that's a beautiful oblation. And, true to our Savior, they're teaching you too. "Unless you become as little children you will never enter the kingdom of heaven."

The Rt. Rev. John S. Thornton
St. Stephen's Episcopal Church
Wimberley, Texas
November 2, 2014

"Bye" To A Friend

Dulles International Airport, Washington, D.C., Tuesday, August 27, 1996

On United Flight 920 from Denver to Washington, D.C., we are in a holding pattern over Peoria for more than an hour. There is bad weather in the Ohio Valley, and planes headed for major eastern airports are stacking up. It makes very little difference how late the plane might be, because I do not have to make a connection in D.C. I am going to take this same plane to London. I can leave my luggage in the overhead bin and get off and walk around the airport for an hour or so before reboarding...As we make our approach, the purser announces that all passengers will have to get off and take their luggage with them...Since I am in the last row (42) of this 777, I am one of the last passengers to get off. I go up the jetway, then through a labyrinth of narrow corridors; and, when I emerge in the waiting area, I am in a throng of impatient and voluble passengers bound for London...There is such a crowd around Gate B-3 that I go to the other side of the concourse to find space for my luggage. I stand there, waiting, watching people coming and going, wistful about this trip to visit my dying friend. Evidently, I look suggestible and compliant. A United agent, a very courteous young man, comes out of nowhere; and, almost nose to nose with me, he points to my luggage and asks, "Is this your luggage?" "That?" I say, also pointing to it. "Yeah, that's my luggage." "Is that all you have?" "That's it," I say. "Only carry-ons, huh?" "That's it," I repeat. Since I know that I do not fit the profile of a skyjacker or bomber, this interrogation puzzles me. But it does not puzzle me very long. The agent says, "Would you like to have a Connoisseur Class seat on a flight leaving for London in five minutes?" "You bet I would," I say. "Then follow me." I follow him to the counter at Gate B-3 and stand nonplussed but exuberant while he punches information into the computer. As he hands me a new boarding pass, I cannot contain my curiosity any longer. "Why are you doing this?" "We need your seat," he says. They have overbooked the flight. So somebody else will get to sit in Seat 42D in Tourist Class on United Flight 920 to London, while I get to sit in seat 6E on United Flight 724. "Get down to Gate B-14 as fast as you can," he says. "They're waiting for you." They are. When I step into the plane, the door is closed behind me; and, within minutes, the 767 is pushed away from the terminal. I am a connoisseur…I have no idea how much a Connoisseur Class ticket costs, but it must cost a lot more than a Tourist Class ticket. From the moment I flop down in that huge leather seat until I wearily struggle out of it at Heathrow the next morning, I am served much and served well. But, for a recovering Calvinist, it really is too much and too well. After seven hours in Seat 6E, I am ready to go back to Seat 42D again. Connoisseur Class is great for my *soma*, but Tourist Class suits my *psyche* better. That is just the way it is with me.

An Inter-city train bound for Crewe, Cheshire, Wednesday, August 28, 1996

The Inter-city train rocks and, on some stretches, rockets toward Crewe, the intermediate stops at Milton Keynes and Rugby. With farming in my blood, I notice the fields on both sides of the train. There are herds of dairy cows, Holsteins and Jerseys. There are herds of beef cattle, Herefords mostly. There are flocks of sheep, Merinos and Romneys, and, possibly, Lincolns, too. I cannot be sure.

White-faced sheep are not as easy to identify at 120 miles an hour as black-and-white or brown cows. The wheat has been harvested; and, in some fields, the straw has been baled, leaving only golden stubble to proclaim the land's unceasing productivity. Some fields have been plowed already. Such an enterprise agriculture is. It is the grinding, but mystical work of a few, the many having gone to cities, as in America…A canal meanders through the fields and villages, and canal boats slip silently, almost wakeless, along it. Tourists can see much of rural England from canal boats…From the station in Rugby, I can see the spire of a church. It is the tallest structure in town. It seems to penetrate the low clouds on this grey day, just as our religion penetrates the mystery of God…Just outside Rugby, there is a new golf course where pastures and wheat fields used to be. It is treeless, pond-less, and sandtrap-less. Excepting for a ball hooked crazily onto the railroad tracks, there is nowhere to lose it…We are coming into Crewe now. It is a rail center and an industrial town. It is where Rolls Royce cars are made. Ten kilometers away, in a little village called Betley in Staffordshire, my friend Donald Nicholl lies dying. I have come all this way, not to meet his needs, but to meet my own. I have to thank him for giving me the courage to try to live as a Christian man and, when my time comes, to try to die as a Christian man…Whenever I am with Donald, the world becomes as large as the cosmos and life becomes as simple as the commands of Jesus.

Rostherne, Common Lane, Betley, Staffordshire, Wednesday, August 28, 1996

I take a double-decker, the C84, from the train station in Crewe to Betley. At the town limits, the sign reads "BETLEY WELCOMES CAREFUL DRIVERS." (By the time drivers think about being careful, they have already driven through this tiny village.) The bus driver lets me off across the road from a pub called "The Swan," and I walk along Newcastle Road a few hundred yards, then cross and walk down Common Lane. Donald and Dorothy live in a small brick house about halfway down. The car is not in the garage; so I know that Dorothy is gone, probably shopping. Donald may be with her. I ring the doorbell. Mary, Donald's and Dorothy's oldest daughter, opens the door and looks at me with a degree of puzzlement. But, when I introduce myself, she grasps my hands and kisses me on the cheek. I know that I am welcome. It is just as Donald said in one of his letters to me: "We have become like brothers, John." As we go into the living room, Mary calls to her father, who is upstairs. In a moment he appears, ducking, necessarily, under the doorway. He is still six feet seven inches tall. We embrace with the awkward tenderness of two men. It is especially awkward for these two, because one of the two (I) is ten inches shorter than the other (he). It is nose to sternum every time. Then he says, "Come with me to my 'dugout'." I follow him upstairs to his library, from which his writing table has been removed and into which a bed has been placed. There he spends his days. In the early afternoon, he and Dorothy nap there. There, with his beloved, he is surrounded by his books and icons and photographs of those who have shaped and reshaped his being over seventy-four years. Among them are St. Francis of Assisi, Mother Teresa of Calcutta, Edith Stein, Charles de Foucauld, Maximillian Colby, David Jones, Ite Gwenallt, St. Seraphim of Sarov and others whose names most of us would not recognize...." Dorothy is the most wonderful woman," he says. "She's the quintessential Martha. I say, 'My love, Martha was so busy doing things that she didn't do the one thing that's really necessary. We just need to be together in these last days.' She's the most wonderful woman." Then, characteristically, he outlines exactly what we will do together for the next three days. We will meet morning and afternoon, for half an hour each time. "I tire so easily," he says. He asks if I would be willing to celebrate the Eucharist for him and Dorothy on Friday afternoon. Without reminding him that he and Dorothy are Roman Catholics and that I am in another Anglican bishop's diocese, a "Yes" burst from my heart. I did not expect that our encounter would come to this kind of closure, completion and Holy Communion. And though he invites me to spend a few minutes with him and Victor and Esther deWaal on Saturday morning, I decline. Though this man is a giant in every way, I cannot drain any more of his energy. "There are two things I must do before I die," he says. "I must prepare myself to go to God, and I must witness to the truth. It isn't easy, but it's simple." Before he can explain what he means by saying that it is simple, he rolls out of bed and gets a copy of Bishop Appleton's little book of prayers off the shelf. He opens it to page 37 and says, "I read this every day."

"Let the healing grace of your love, O Lord, so transform me that I may play my part in the transfiguration of the world. From a place of suffering, death and corruption to a realm of infinite light, joy and love. Make me so obedient to your Spirit that my life may become a living prayer and a witness to your unfailing presence."

- MARTIN ISRAEL

"It's good that you've come, John," he says. "I keep thinking of those words in the Transfiguration story. 'It's good that we're here.' But it can be good only if it's at my pace." Knowing this man as I do, I know that my time is up. Excepting it is not up. Again, he rolls out of bed and gets a new copy of *Holiness* off the shelf. "The American version doesn't have the 'Epilogue' in it. It's important. And I want to write in it before you leave." Then, getting down on his knees, he slips a little book from between two large ones on the lowest shelf. "Over the years," he says, "this has been a great help to me." The book is titled *The Witness of Edith Barfoot: The Joyful Vocation to Suffering.* "I want you to take this," he says. "Now come with me." I follow him into the bedroom, where papers and cassettes are neatly arranged on the window bench. "It's kind of eerie," he says. "This is the way they're supposed to be after I die." Again, he gets down on his knees and picks out three cassettes titled "West Riding Childhood," talks he did for the BBC. Then he gives me the manuscript for his new book titled *The Triumphs of the Spirit in Russia*, about St. Seraphim of Sarov, Nikolai Fyodorov, Fyodor Dostoevsky and Lev Tolstoy. Darton, Longman and Todd will publish it soon in the U.K. and Orbis simultaneously in the U.S. Sensing his fatigue, both of body and mind, I thank him. Stooping over, he kisses me on both cheeks and says, "Bye now. See you tomorrow." I let myself out the kitchen door and walk up Common Lane, lightly burdened with the learning, the wisdom, and the revelations of this astonishing man.

The Hand and Trumpet Inn, Betley, Staffordshire, Thursday, August 29, 1996

I will see Donald again this morning, sometime between 10:30 and 10:45. I have to prepare myself. With Donald, there is no small talk. He demands veracity in communication and rectitude in action. Every word is supposed to increase our understanding of each other and of humankind and of God, and every action must promote "the restoration of all things." Though I always sense the broad, the boundless, kindliness and forgivingness of this man, there is a severity in his standards. It is similar to the severity of the Old Testament prophets. It is the severity, I suspect, of Jesus. And one has to have done his homework. "There's no substitute for knowing," he always says. Furthermore, he will not tolerate gossip. If you say anything that verges on *loshon hora* (evil speech), get ready for a rebuke. It will be the last one you will ever get from him; because, thereafter and forever, you will rebuke yourself – to avoid his. Though we usually do not deliberately slander each other, still, as the old rabbis used to say, we are all covered with "the dust of slander." So I get ready to walk the mile or so to Donald's and Dorothy's house. I am, by prayer, trying to cleanse my heart for this brief, but eternal, encounter.

Rostherne, Common Lane, Betley, Staffordshire, Thursday, August 29, 1996

I ring the doorbell. Dorothy answers. Even as she closes the door behind us, she says, "Would you like tea and scones?" Tea and scones seems always to be available. But it is the availability of her genuine concern for others that makes one marvel. Politely declining tea and scones, I climb the stairs to Donald's "dugout." Donald is lying on the bed, looking weary after a sleepless night. Before we speak, Dorothy comes in, with tea and scones. There is no stopping her. Donald could have predicted this. Still, being able to predict it, he just watches in amazement, the same amazement he felt when they met in grammar school over sixty years ago. As she leaves the room, he points at her and shakes his head, as if to say, Can you believe the goodness of this woman? "Today, John, we're going to do two things. First, we're going to say the 'Our Father,' then we're going to sit in silence." And that is what we do. We say the "Our Father," then we sit in silence. I say a prayer of thanksgiving for our friendship. He concludes with what, under the circumstances, could only be described as jubilation. "This is the day that the Lord has made," he says. "Let us rejoice and be glad in it." Then, looking straight at me, he adds, "It's grace, John. It's all grace." He has a stack of books ready for me to take back to my room at The Hand and Trumpet Inn. Each contains an essay he wrote. I am glad for each one of them, glad for the burden of them as I go downstairs. Since I want them all for my collection of his works, it makes sense to take them to Crewe for photocopying. I put them all into one of Dorothy's shopping bags, kiss her goodbye, and walk up Common Lane to wait for the C84 to stop across the road from "The Swan."

Rostherne, Common Lane, Betley, Staffordshire, Thursday, August 29, 1996

As agreed upon, I return at 4:00 pm. I have a bunch of flowers for Dorothy. They were in a bucket by the gate in front of a house in the village. The sign read "Flowers 75p." One must always have an oblation for this continual eucharist called life. Donald and Dorothy are both in the kitchen. Scones are on a rack on the counter, cooling, coaxing more indulgence. We decide to stay right there, letting the scones be the incense of our evening sacrifice of gratitude for all the good things we are experiencing. Donald is in a jovial and, so it seems to me, mischievous mood. Dorothy, while arranging the flowers in a vase, asks if I had gotten them at a particular house on Newcastle Road. When I say that I did, she tells me a story about the people who live in that house. Donald grins and says, "Why is it, John, that some rogues are so likeable and some very good people are such a pain in the neck?" "The answer is simple," I say. "It's to keep you permanently befuddled." Probably because I refer to the speed at which drivers drive through Betley, our conversation turns to the pace at which we live, both in the U.K. and in the U.S. "It reminds me of something Cardinal Hume once said," Donald says. "'It isn't true that our contemporaries are wicked; they're just crazy.'" The scones on the plate gone and more refused, we go upstairs to Donald's "dugout." He lies down on the bed, folds his hands, closes his eyes and...In silence he lies and I sit for half an hour, until the deepest peace is ended by the repeated ringing of the doorbell. "See you tomorrow," I say, then leave, encountering two clergymen, one Roman Catholic, one Anglican, already drinking tea and eating scones in the kitchen.

The Hand and Trumpet, Betley, Staffordshire, Friday, August 30, 1996

At 2:00 a.m. (7:00 p.m. Boise time) I am wide awake. The dawn – if there will be a dawn today – is hours away. I have seen the sun only several times in the past four days. Sleep is both impossible and unnecessary. I feel, strangely, rested and ready for activity. The options are to listen to more of the cassettes Donald gave me, though that might interrupt the sleep of the guests in adjacent rooms, or to read. Since I have to return the manuscript of *The Triumphs of the Spirit in Russia* this afternoon, I decide to read the last chapter on the theme of *sobornost* in the works of Fyodor Dostoevsky. As I read, I reflect on a couple of things that Dostoevsky said:

"The most important thing in the world is spontaneous compassion. As for justice, that is a secondary matter."

"You must know that there is nothing higher or stronger or sounder or more useful afterwards in life than some good memory, especially a memory from childhood, from the parental home. You hear a lot said about your education, yet some beautiful, sacred memory, preserved through childhood, is perhaps the best education. If a man stores up many such memories to take into life, then he is saved for his whole life. And if only memory remains with us in our hearts, that alone may serve some day for our salvation."

I fall asleep and awake to a dawnless day.

Rostherne, Common Lane, Betley, Staffordshire, Friday, August 30, 1996

I knock on the kitchen door, then let myself in, softly calling, "Dorothy." She is right there, in the kitchen, fixing tea. "Donald is waiting for you," she says. "Go right up." I do. She follows, with tea and scones. As she puts the tray down on the table next to my chair, she mentions some national controversy. He gives her that look, that look full of affection and gratitude and humor. "Given my condition, Love," he says, "I'm not into controversies anymore." She gives him that same look, that look full of affection and gratitude and humor, then adds, "Right." Maybe she is wondering what I am wondering: How could this man ever stay out of controversies? It will take death to stop him. Everything he writes for *The Tablet* is either in response to a controversy or the cause of one. It is just not possible for him to be disinterested in and, though in pain, dispassionate about the pain of others. The work of reconciliation ends with one's last breath and, in the providence of God, does not end then. My thoughts and any further conversation end with the ringing of the doorbell. It is the hospice nurse. After meeting her, I leave, taking more articles to be photocopied at Prontoprint in Crewe. One of those articles is titled "Rich Man, Poor Man," about the Church's prohibition of usury for more than a thousand years. It contains the following statement: "We now find ourselves in the situation where the only sizeable group propagating the ancient Catholic teaching on usury consists of Muslims." Did that start a controversy in England! And it is not likely to end with Donald's death. To some, going back to the Church's teaching about usury will seem anachronistic and ridiculous; to others, it will seem prophetic and maybe the best way to reconcile the peoples of the First World and the Third.

Rostherne, Common Lane, Betley, Staffordshire, Saturday, August 31, 1996

Again, I let myself in the kitchen door. Dorothy hears me and rushes to the kitchen. We make a few last-minute preparations for the celebration of the Eucharist in the dining room. When everything is ready, I go up to Donald's "dugout." Few words are said. We both feel the need for silence and, at my suggestion, agree that after the Eucharist, we all kiss and I will leave for good. Though hard, it seems best. We go downstairs to join Dorothy in the dining room. In spite of the pain of the impending separation by my departure and Donald's death, resurrection is in the air. I read a page from *The Rise and Progress of Religion in the Soul* by Philip Doddridge (published 1853):

"And, now to enlarge on this copious Head, "*reflect* once more, *how your Affections stand* with Regard to *this World* and *another.* Are you more deeply and practically *convinced* of the *Vanity of these Things which are seen*, and *are Temporal?* Do you perceive *your Expectations from them*, and *your Attachment to them, to diminish?* You are *willing to stay* in this World, *as long as your Father pleases;* and it is *right* and *well*; But do you and *your Bond so loosened to it*, that you are *willing*, heartily willing, *to leave it at the shortest Warning*, so that if God should see fit to *summon you away on a sudden*, though it should be in the Midst of your Enjoyment's Pursuits, Expectations, and Hopes, you would *cordially consent to the Remove;* without saying 'Lord, let me stay a *little while longer*, to enjoy this or that agreeable Entertainment, to finish this or that Scheme?' Can you *think* with an habitual *Calmness* and hearty *Approbation*, if such be the Divine Pleasure, *of waking no more* when you lie down on your Bed, *of returning Home no more* when you go out of your House? And yet, on the other hand, how *great* soever the *Burthens of Life* are, do you find a *Willingness to bear them*, in Submission to the Will of your Heavenly Father, though it should be *to many future Years;* and though they should be *Years of far greater Affliction*, than you have ever yet seen? Can you say *calmly* and *steadily*, if not with such Overflowings of *tender Affections* as you could desire, 'Behold, *thy Servant, thy Child*, is in Thine Hand, do *with me as seemeth good in thy Sight! My Will is melted into Thine;* to be *here* or *there*, in *this* or *that Circumstance*, just as Thou pleases and as shall *best suit* with Thy *great extensive Plan*, which it is *impossible* that *I* or all *the Angels in heaven* should *mend.*"

The bread and wine are consecrated. We eat and drink. We hold hands and pray. We hold hands for a long time, but we know we must let go. Finally, we do. We kiss. I leave, feeling bereft as I walk up Common Lane.

Ironbridge, Staffordshire, Saturday, August 31, 1996

Determined not to return to Donald's and Dorothy's house and interrupt the visits of family members, I decide to go to Ironbridge, where the world's oldest iron bridge still stands. On a map, it does not look far away; but there is no direct route, and I make up my mind to go, which I do, by bus to Crewe, by train to Wolverhampton, by train to Telford, by bus to Ironbridge. A little more than three hours away from The Hand and Trumpet Inn, I am standing under a masterpiece. It is not big, because the River Severn, which it spans, is not wide. Its very smallness allows me to contemplate the intricate simplicity of its design. Its lightness and fragility are only apparent. This bridge has stood for centuries and has endured the periodic flooding of the Severn. Today, Ironbridge is a World Heritage Site, which makes it a "tourist trap." Still, it is a lovely place; and its loveliness is not ruined by the huge nuclear power plant only a mile or so away. It was nature, asserting that "dearest freshness deep down things," that restored Ironbridge after it was ravaged and raped at the beginning of the Industrial Revolution. While the iron industry was there, a few families, particularly the Darbys, became rich and built mansions to herald both their prosperity and their piety. (They were devout Quakers.) The masses who worked in the coal and ironstone mines and in the tar pits under appalling and inhumane conditions, well, they had to endure such squalor as only

Charles Dickens could describe. There were no wells from which pure water could be pumped. They got their drinking and cooking water from the Severn. For lack of a sanitation system, excepting for gutters and gullies, it was not long before the Severn was a cesspool stretching to the Irish Sea. In the midst of all that inventiveness and industry, of which the iron bridge was the symbol, cholera destroyed thousands of lives, men's, women's and children's. On this trip, I see a lot of a small part of England, particularly Cheshire, Staffordshire and Shropshire; and I see a lot of English people, particularly those who use public transportation; and I drink a lot of English tea, which is uniformly good. And I notice the billboards in the train stations. There is one I see in every station, and I am transfixed by it every time. The British Red Cross sponsors it. On the top half is a photograph of an African boy who is crawling along a dirt road. His right leg is so mangled that it is hardly distinguishable as a leg. It is a useless appendage. On the bottom half is the following statement: "AND YOU THINK YOU'VE GOT A DIFFICULT JOURNEY TO WORK. Landmines must be stopped." This very day, I read about a young Englishman named Chris Howes, who was murdered by the Khmer Rouge in Cambodia. He was a former military officer and an expert in clearing landmines. With twenty-eight other volunteers for Mines Advisory Group in London, he went to Cambodia to help rid the country of landmines. While there, the Khmer Rouge kidnapped him and all the other volunteers. He was the only one, probably because he was a munitions expert, whom they did not release. When he refused to cooperate in their demand for ransom, they shot him. His father, who was interviewed by *The Times*, said something that seems true, so true that it accounts for cowards as it accounts for the courage of a few. "My boy went out there to save lives and ended paying with his own. There are hundreds of people out there in Cambodia with their arms and legs intact who wouldn't have if it wasn't for my son." It reminded me of something Father Pavel Florensky said just before the NKVD executed him in 1937. Father Florensky, who was a Russian Orthodox priest and poet and historian and philosopher and mathematician and physicist and engineer and inventor and iconographer, was called "the Russian Leonardo da Vinci." (Donald Nicholl wrote an article about him titled "One of a Great Cloud of Witnesses: Father Pavel Florensky.") As the punishment for his crime, which was to have a radiant faith in the Trinity, he was sent from gulag to gulag and finally executed. Shortly before his execution, he wrote the following: "The universe is so organized that only at the price of suffering and persecution can the world be given anything. That is the law of life, its fundamental axiom. Greatness must pay for its gift in blood." (*The Secret Files from the Literary Archives of the KGB.*) I think of Jesus, on the cross. I think also of the risen Lord and that "great cloud of witnesses," including Father Pavel Florensky and Chris Hawes. Though one train is cancelled and another delayed, I get back to The Hand and Trumpet Inn by 6:45 p.m. Richard Nicholl, Donald's and Dorothy's son, and I will have dinner at 7:15 p.m.

Betley, Staffordshire, Sunday, September 1, 1996

At breakfast, I am reminded once again that "a little child shall lead them." An English girl named Sarah, maybe seven or eight years old, comes to breakfast ahead of her parents. She makes the round of tables. When she comes to mine, she says, "I know where you're from." "You do?" I say. "Where am I from?" "You're from America," she says. "You're right – but how did you know?" Without having to think about how she might phrase it, she says, "By the way you speak." Yes, it is by the way I – all of us – speak. And some English people say it is by the way we walk. In any case, we cannot hide ourselves in England. We are who we are...I pay my bill and thank the pub owners, who have fulfilled the laws of hospitality in both Torah and Gospel. They even offer to drive me to the village church, but I insist that I need the walk. And I do need it, both for exercise and contemplation. With a heavy suitcase in one hand and a canvas bag full of books in the other, I walk slowly past the Betley Court Farms pastures, past the soccer field, past the cricket pitch, past the abandoned Methodist church, then up "The Butts." The bells of St. Margaret's Church fill the empty air with hymnody. And, though the faithful have been awake for several hours, the bells surely awaken their faith and summon many to the sacrifice of thanksgiving. I walk through the graveyard, where there are a few new gravestones and many old, names and dates and epitaphs eroded through eras of history, then up the stone steps and into the church that was built some time in the Late Eighteenth Century. The Vicar greets me, and we talk about Donald's condition for a while. I ask him if there is someone who might take me to the train station in Crewe after the service, since the C84 runs only every two hours on Sunday. He says that he is sure that there is and will ask. Habitually, I sit in a pew on the right side of the aisle. The cold and musty building, especially the faded stained-glass windows, make me think about history and of the gift that we call Anglicanism. While making one proud, it can take away one's pride, too. By comparison to what we have been given, we cannot give very much in our lifetime, even if we give all. In a place like this, one becomes a thanks-giver and resolves to become a life-giver for the sake of the present generation and those who will come after us....I realize what a privilege it is to sit in the nave, to be one of the congregation, and not be in charge. It is a privilege clergy, because of their vocation, have to forego....St. Margaret's is definitely a "low church;" but, when there are so many unrehearsed and unrehearsable epiphanies of the Spirit in a place, "low" and "high" are really silly judgments. The only judgment one should ever make is of himself. Am I ready to receive Christ however he offers himself to me? When the Vicar asks if anyone would be willing to drive the Bishop of Idaho to the train station in Crewe, a tall, thin, bald man standing in the third row on the left side of the aisle raises his hand. I have a ride.

En route to the train station in Crewe, Cheshire, Sunday, September 1, 1996

The tall, thin bald man is Geoffrey Bell. His wife is Peggy. At age 82, Geoffrey is a semi-retired solicitor. He still goes to his office in the largest law firm in Newcastle-under-Lyme every day, but his only job is to manage the estates of the Wedgewood heirs. He has outlived them all. I suspect that he does his job meticulously. As we pull into the semi-circular drive in front of the train station, Geoffrey wants me to know that he has not always gone to church. Like most Englishmen, he was baptized in the Church of England. And, like most, he did not take part in the Holy Mysteries for most of his life. However, he has been taking part for the past eight years – because, eight years ago, he was very ill, and nearly everyone expected him to die. But he did not die. Miraculously, he recovered. "I think it's because of my wife," he says. "I discovered that she was going to church every day to pray for me." He chokes up. A tear wells up in his eye. There is silence for the first time. It is good that a man knows that his life depends on the ministrations and intercessions of others. We grasp hands, all three of us. Peggy, who has not uttered one word in ten kilometers, says, "Bye." Angels are not very talkative. I rush down the stairs to Platform 5, to catch the 1:03 to London and, in a day, a plane back to the U.S.

Grace At Table(S)

(Bishop Thornton offered the following "Grace" at the banquet to honor The Rt. Rev. James Waggoner, who, earlier in the day, was consecrated Bishop of the Diocese of Spokane.)

"O God, subtle and insinuating Holy Spirit, making Yourself obvious and unmistakable and, to use a word these people use, incarnate, then, in an instant, vanishing again.... Anyway, O God, Holy Spirit, we thank You for coming this evening. We know You're here. You always come to these things. If You aren't here, it would be the first time since, well, since banquets began. Now make us guess who You are.

Was it You who just smiled and said 'Hello' to that quiet, shy woman on Your right?

Was it You who just threw Your arms around that horrified, but now happy, man on Your left?

Was it You who just told that funny story and made everyone at Your table pound it so hard that the glassware rumbled and collided in clinks?

Was it You who just picked up on that woman's pain, sensed that man's sadness, took her, took him by the hand and made, for the moment, all things well?

Was it You?

Make us guess - and make us never stop guessing. And as we eat this bread and drink this wine and talk with each other about the Law and the Prophets and Jim Waggoner and the Mets and the Yankees and the antic glory of this antic creation, slowly reveal Yourself to us as the lover, the shameless and carefree and jubilant lover of all that and all whom the Father loves and has since the world began. And, O God, since it is reasonably expected of me, may I ask that You bless this food to our use and us to Christ's service from this moment until we serve You in heaven.

Amen."

The Rt. Rev. John S. Thornton
Davenport Hotel
Spokane, Washington
October 23, 2000

Did You See Him In The '60s?

The creeds of Man are
Penciled on restroom walls,
Chalked on sidewalks,
Painted on traffic signs,
Jack-knifed into theater seats,
Pinned on lapels,
Glued to rear bumpers.
Sometimes, they are a lamentation;
Sometimes, an exultation;
Always, a declaration:
Here I stand.
One of the best of the '60s is
"God isn't dead —
He just doesn't want to get involved."
That says so much about
Man's faith
And lack of it.
The faithless believer — of whom there are many — might say,
Sure,
I believe in God,
Father, Son, and Holy Spirit, too,
The whole thing —
But what difference does it make?
The difference is between
Seeing and not seeing,
Hearing and not hearing,

+John S. Thornton

Being alive and wishing you were dead.
Assent to the ancient formulation,
Three in one,
One in three,
May help in getting through liturgies,
But not in getting through life;
And life is what there is to get through –
And get with!
I –
[I, myself,
Or, if I were you] –
I would not ask,
Do you believe in God?
Everybody does;
Nobody wants to be unpatriotic.
What I want to know is this:
Did you see Him,
Did you hear Him,
Did you, at the very least, read about Him,
As He was creating worlds *ex nihilo*
And electing
And blessing
And disciplining
And cursing
And incarnating Himself in human form
In the '60s?
Did you?
If you did not,
You just missed one whole decade of
The Mysterium Tremendum's extravaganza

Called "History."
He was involved in all that,
Making
And remaking
And unmaking to make all over again
A world He loves
With a love young lovers would be embarrassed by.
Perhaps His providence was too obvious – and too good to be true;
Perhaps it was hidden in the supposed insignificance of everyday
things.

II

Now the '60s are gone,
Ten years,
One hundred and twenty months,
Three thousand six hundred and fifty-three days
Of good and evil
Chronicled in chronicles
Ten cents each, twenty-five cents on Sunday.
Headlines and fillers too,
Announcing what we did
With
And for
And to
Each other *anno Domini*.
Because of what we did to each other,
We have learned a little more about
The history and geography of folly and vengeance:
Prague…

Chicago…
East Berlin…
Palomares…
Owerri…
Watts…
Salisbury…
Selma…
My Lai…
Dallas, Memphis, and Los Angeles…
Jerusalem…
Dugway Proving Grounds…
Havanna…
White Sands Missile Range…
Santa Barbara…
Et al.
The "et al." is important –
It probably includes our hometowns.
Since AP and UPI did not,
We did not notice much wrong, either;
Though much wrong there must have been.
I doubt that the human race completed the lexicon of horrors,
To which St. Paul gave the title "Principalities and Powers of Darkness;"
But we gave some new meanings to some old words,
Like
Slavery,
Tyranny,
Assassination,
Atrocity,
Genocide,

Pollution…
In a moment of calculated [and calculating] penitence,
We could wish for the publication of
An expurgated and abridged record of our deeds in the '60s.
Perhaps our children's children need never know
What destructiveness their grandparents were capable of.
We might look good
Even though we were not.
Kyrie eleison!
Write that on the blackboard of your mind
Three thousand six hundred and fifty-three times.

III

Still,
Someone waved and shouted for recognition.
Now I know that God is,
As I know that the Sun shall rise,
An uncanny and inexpressible knowing;
Though He still eludes and defies me
[And, I suppose, you, too].
I have said, jesting,
This much I am quite sure of:
God loves surprises,
God hates pastels,
And Styrofoam is the invention of God's adversary, the Devil.
In the fourth decade of my life,
I learned one more thing:
God goes through history
As if it were a masquerade party.

He puts on costumes and faces
And makes us guess who He is.
Was that Albert Schweitzer
Or the *Spiritus Creator* in disguise?
Was that Martin Buber?
U Thant?
Paul Tillich?
Malcolm X?
Rachel Carson?
Martin Luther King?
Alexander Dubček?
Pope John XXIII?
Kenneth Skelton?
Jim Ryan?
John Kennedy?
Art Hoppe?
Neil Armstrong?
Kilmer Myers?
Godfrey Canbridge?
Fred Shepler?
And millons of unheralded others,
From den mothers to criminal lawyers,
Or the *Spiritus Creator* in disguise?
Al last,
At long last,
I think I have guessed His identity.
When you reflect and reminisce about
The madness and miracle-working of the '60s,
Do not forget what God and Man, cooperating, did:
The Pill,

The Czechoslavakian resistance,
The human heart transplants,
The 3:51.1 mile,
Pacem in Terris,
The laser,
The German measles vaccine,
The Moon landings,
Silent Spring,
The DNA molecule's decoding,
The Peace Movement,
Boston City Hall,
Laugh-In,
The *War Requiem,*
Project Head Start,
And Lyndon Johnson's resignation.
It was quite a decade!
After we have done our penance,
Perhaps we should rejoice.
Ave Maria!
And Joseph, too!
The spirit of your son
Accomplished some mighty wonders in the '60s.

The Rev. John S. Thornton
Christ Episcopal Church
Sausalito, California
Late '60s

Archimedes

Little Archimedes was a curious kid;
he had an ego, a superego and a very strong id.

He wanted answers, wanted them now,
wanted to know why, wanted to know how.

He jumped in the bathtub as naked as we,
yelled, Eureka!, the volume splashed out equals the volume of me.

For a small fry, that young Greek
was a brainchild, a genius, an upcoming geek.

His mom was, of pies, the Athenian queen,
made fruit pies even Socrates hadn't seen.

Eyeing a pie, that boy, in a tone so profound,
asked what it measured, not only across, but all around.

How would I know? his mother laughed.
Ask your dad; he's the smart one, the inventor, the philomath.

The Egyptians, the Babylonians couldn't figure it out, he said.
Why not forget it and just go to bed?

Not little Archy. He was obsessed with that pie;
he wouldn't give up; he'd try and he'd try.

He pondered that pie 'til the dang thing grew stale,
then cried, Eureka!, my theorem won't ever fail.

Measure the pie from center to edge, he'd roar;
then square that number and multiply by three point one four.

Easy! So that, of a pie, whether modest or immense,
is the distance around, called the circumference.

Archy's mom and Archy's dad, though mightily pleased, said,
Now just eat your pie and go to bed.

The Rt. Rev. John S. Thornton
St. Michael's Cathedral
Lenten Lunch
Boise, Idaho
March 27, 2015

A Blessing

I bless your eyes, that you may see God's image in everyone.

I bless your ears, that you may hear the cry of the poor.

I bless your lips, that you may speak nothing but the Gospel of Jesus.

I bless your hands, that everything you receive and everything you give may be a sacrament.

I bless your feet, that you may run to those who need you.

The Rev. John S. Thornton
Taucross Farm
Scio, Oregon
1985

The first three blessings are adapted from Godric by Frederick Buechner and the last two written by then Father Thornton, all based on ancient Orthodox tradition.